Withdrawn

MISSION:
ELEPHANT RESCUE

An elephant tosses water in Samburu National Reserve in Kenya. Elephants return to their favorite water holes to drink, cool off, and play.

MISSION: ELEPHANT RESCUE

ALL ABOUT ELEPHANTS AND HOW TO SAVE THEM

ASHLEE BROWN BLEWETT WITH NATIONAL GEOGRAPHIC EXPLORER DANIEL RAVEN-ELLISON

NATIONAL GEOGRAPHIC KiDS

WASHINGTON, D.C.

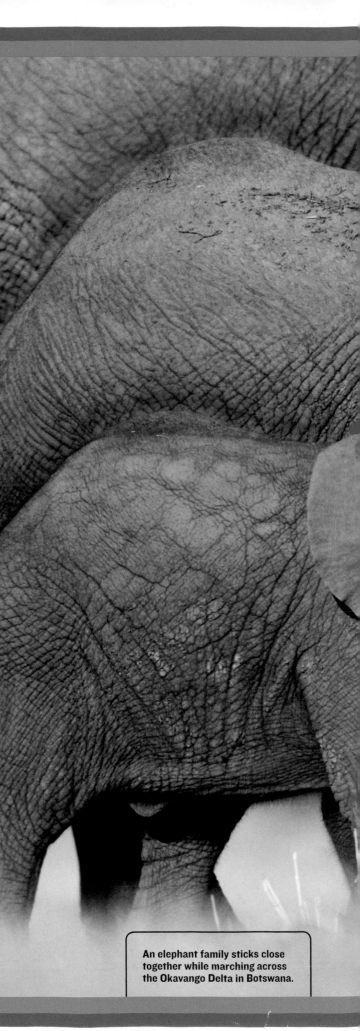

>> CONTENTS

An elephant family sticks close together while marching across the Okavango Delta in Botswana.

MISSION: ANIMAL RESCUE

Save ANIMALS >> Save the WORLD

Mission: Animal Rescue includes books, a *National Geographic Kids* magazine feature, Web resources, and more—plus videos! Check out kids.nationalgeographic.com/mission-animal-rescue for more information!

MISSION: ANIMAL RESCUE

At National Geographic we know how much you care about animals. They enrich our planet—and our lives. Habitat loss, hunting, and other human activities are threatening many animals across the globe. The loss of these animals is a loss to humanity. They have a right to our shared planet and deserve to be protected.

With your help, we can save animals—through education, through habitat protection, and through a network of helping hands. I firmly believe the animals of the world will be safer with us on their side.

Throughout this book and the other books in the Mission: Animal Rescue series, you'll see animal rescue activities just for kids. If you go online at kids.nationalgeographic.com/mission-animal-rescue, you can join a community of kids who want to help animals as much as you do. Look for animal rescue videos, chats with explorers, and more. Plus, don't miss the dramatic stories of animal rescues in *National Geographic Kids* magazine.

We share our Earth with animals. Helping them means helping our planet and protecting our future. Together we can do it.

—Daniel Raven-Ellison, *Guerrilla Geographer and National Geographic Explorer*

YOUR PURCHASE SUPPORTS ANIMALS AND THEIR HABITATS

The National Geographic Society is a nonprofit organization whose net proceeds support vital exploration, conservation, research, and education programs. Proceeds from this book will go toward the Society's efforts to support animals and their habitats. From building bomas for big cats to protect their wild territory to studying elephants and how they communicate to exploring wild places to better understand animal habitats, National Geographic's programs help save animals and our world. Thank you for your passion and dedication to this cause. To make an additional contribution in support of Mission: Animal Rescue, ask your parents to consider texting ANIMAL to 50555 to give ten dollars. See page 112 for more information.

>>INTRODUCTION

HELP SAVE THE ELEPHANT

Most of us have heard the trumpet blast of an elephant—either in person or recorded—and know how stirring that wild call can sound. Like humans, elephants are social animals. They communicate constantly with other elephants, using many sounds and gestures to say something as simple as "Let's go" or as important as "Help!"

Elephants and humans have a long, complicated history. Elephants have played an important role in human cultures for thousands of years. Some ancient cultures respected elephants and even worshipped them as religious icons. But even though people revered elephants, they also captured them and kept them as pets. Some civilizations put elephants on display in big cities. Others trained them to haul heavy loads or carry troops into battle.

Elephants are no longer trained as war animals, but today they face new battles. Though some cultures still worship elephant gods, elephants are often mistreated. They are captured from the wild and trained to carry tourists through national parks. They are even paraded through city streets during religious festivals. But the situation gets worse. Human settlements are pushing elephants into smaller habitats and thousands are killed every year for their ivory tusks.

Elephants need our help. Across the globe, scientists, conservationists, and people like you are spreading the word about the challenges elephants face and the steps we can take to help. The more of us that join together to educate others, the more success we'll have protecting these majestic animals.

At the end of each chapter in this book, you'll find rescue challenges. By doing these activities, you'll learn more about elephants and the daily struggles they face. You will also help share the message about the importance of the world's largest land animal. Let out a loud trumpet blast and read on to learn how you can make your voice heard. Let's save elephants!

HUMAN DEMAND FOR RELIGIOUS FIGURES AND TRINKETS CARVED FROM IVORY IS THE BIGGEST DRIVER OF ELEPHANT POACHING TODAY.

THE HEAVIEST AFRICAN ELEPHANT TUSK WEIGHED 226.4 POUNDS (102.7 KG).

A herd of elephants gathers on the plains. Elephants are social animals that prefer to be around other elephants.

>>THROUGH AN ELEPHANT'S EYES

Zongoloni, a brave elephant calf, spreads her ears wide and charges into the darkness. Nearby, hyenas whoop and screech, and lion roars echo across the hot, dry savanna in Kenya, a country in eastern Africa. The calf returns to her mother's side, rumbling and nudging her to get up. It has been nearly two days since Zongoloni's mother collapsed in a thicket of thorny trees. The calf is frightened. She is hungry and thirsty, but her mother has no more strength. The elephant simply cannot stand.

A NARROW ESCAPE

Two weeks earlier, a band of poachers invaded the elephants' habitat and shot Zongoloni's mother in the shoulder. The poachers were after the adult elephant's long ivory tusks, or teeth. Ivory tusks are worth a lot of money to criminals who buy them illegally and then sell them as carved sculptures and jewelry.

Zongoloni and her mother narrowly escaped the poachers, but the wound from the bullet was deep. Over the next couple of weeks, the calf's mother grew weaker until she collapsed on the dusty earth. Soon, she will die.

Without the protection and the nourishing milk her mother provides, Zongoloni, at only 18 months old, will

A greedy Zongoloni reaches for a bottle of milk held by one of her keepers.

not survive. Luckily, patrolling humans from a nearby ranch discover the wounded elephant and her calf and call for help.

HELP ARRIVES

Several caring men in green jumpsuits arrive on the scene. The men are from the Kenya Wildlife Service and the David Sheldrick Wildlife Trust, a wildlife conservation organization. Together they form a joint anti-poaching unit.

The men approach Zongoloni, but the aggressive calf fiercely protects her dying mother. One of the men shoots Zongoloni in her side with a pink dart filled with medicine. Several minutes later, Zongoloni lies down on the earth next to her mother and falls asleep.

The men move around the calf and together they lift her limp, heavy body into the back of a truck. They drive off over the bumpy terrain toward a waiting airplane at a nearby airstrip. On the airplane, the dehydrated calf receives life-saving fluids. An hour and a half later, the plane lands at Zongoloni's new home: the elephant orphanage at the David Sheldrick Wildlife Trust in Kenya's Nairobi National Park.

NEW BEGINNINGS

While Zongoloni is still groggy from the medicine, a team of keepers from the orphanage leads the calf into her own wooden stockade, or enclosure, and feeds her a bottle of milk. Three other orphaned calves—Vuria, Faraja, and Jasiri—pad over to greet the new arrival. They rumble softly toward Zongoloni.

The other orphans seem to calm the frightened calf, but as the medicine wears off, Zongoloni becomes aggressive toward the keepers. She charges at any human that tries to approach her. This is probably because she sees all humans as dangerous poachers like the ones who shot her mother.

Over the next several days, Zongoloni grieves the loss of her mother, just like a human grieves the loss of a loved one. She continues to charge at the keepers, but, fortunately, they are able to get her to eat. She munches on the leafy branches inside the stockade and drinks milk from a bucket that the keepers place near the bars of her enclosure.

Every morning, the other orphans walk over to Zongoloni's enclosure to greet the calf. She watches intently as they slurp milk from oversize bottles held by the keepers. The keepers hope this will show Zongoloni that they are caring humans, not dangerous poachers. Zongoloni also watches the other orphaned calves form a line twice a day and follow the keepers into the meadows and thickets that surround the orphanage. And every afternoon they return, safe and sound.

Finally, nearly two weeks after her arrival at the orphanage, Zongoloni stops charging at humans. She accepts milk from a bottle again, and she is allowed out of her enclosure to follow the other calves into the forest for their midday mud bath at the large, shimmering water hole.

At first, the keepers are afraid that Zongoloni might try to run away, but to their surprise, the calf quickly

(Above) Rescuers try to calm Zongoloni. (Top right) Zongoloni plays with her new friends. (Right) Guests glimpse elephants being bottle-fed by the orphanage's keepers.

settles into the routine. She has learned by now that the keepers are caring people who will protect her. That night, Zongoloni settles into a new stable. A keeper tucks a blanket around the elephant and sleeps alongside her, waking every few hours to feed and comfort the calf.

With each new day, Zongoloni becomes more comfortable with the keepers and her new elephant friends. Before long, she splashes alongside the other orphans at the water hole as if she has always known them. She joins in the fun, chasing impalas and warthogs away from the water hole and "bush bashing," or tossing her head back and forth and charging through the bushes to create noise and commotion.

Though Zongoloni tragically lost her mother and had to be rescued by humans, a new elephant family adopted her. The older orphans will teach her how to be an elephant—something her mother would have done. And some day, when she is able to take care of herself, Zongoloni will roam wild again across the savannas of southern Kenya.

THE DAVID SHELDRICK WILDLIFE TRUST RESCUES AND RAISES ORPHANED RHINOS, TOO.

CHAPTER I

>> TOWERING TITANS

"ELEPHANTS HAVE GOT ATTITUDE. AT THE SAME TIME, THEY ARE THE GENTLE GIANTS OF AFRICA."

—DERECK JOUBERT, NATIONAL GEOGRAPHIC EXPLORER-IN-RESIDENCE

This broken-tusked African elephant stands tall and fans its ears. Flared ears are a sign of an unhappy elephant.

Elephants are one of Earth's last true giants. The towering titans meander across open savannas, explore thick forests, and march across sandy deserts as the largest living land animals on the planet. No other animal comes close.

LAND GIANTS

Adult male elephants outweigh white rhinos—the second largest animal on Earth—by as much as 8,000 pounds (3,629 kg). From the size of their bodies to the impact they have on their habitats, everything about elephants is big.

Elephants belong to the Elephantidae family. Today three species, or types, of elephant live in Africa and Asia: African savanna and forest elephants (*Loxodonta africana* and *Loxodonta cyclotis*) and Asian elephants (*Elephas maximus*). Except for a few physical traits that set the species apart, African and Asian elephants are quite similar.

Elephants are mammals, which means they are warm-blooded and have hair on their bodies. Females give birth to live young and feed their babies milk they produce themselves. At birth they weigh as much as an adult human man! Every year they grow bigger and stronger.

POWERFUL PACHYDERMS

Wild elephants can live to be 70 years old. The oldest and largest males can reach 13 feet (4 m) tall and weigh over 13,000 pounds (5,897 kg). That's about the weight of two Land Rover jeeps stacked on top of each other! Females can be nine feet (3 m) tall, and they weigh about half as much as males. Still, even a female elephant could kill an animal—including a

AN ELEPHANT CAN SUCK UP TO 2 GALLONS (8 L) OF WATER INTO ITS TRUNK AT ONE TIME.

An elephant charges when startled by gunshots fired at poachers.

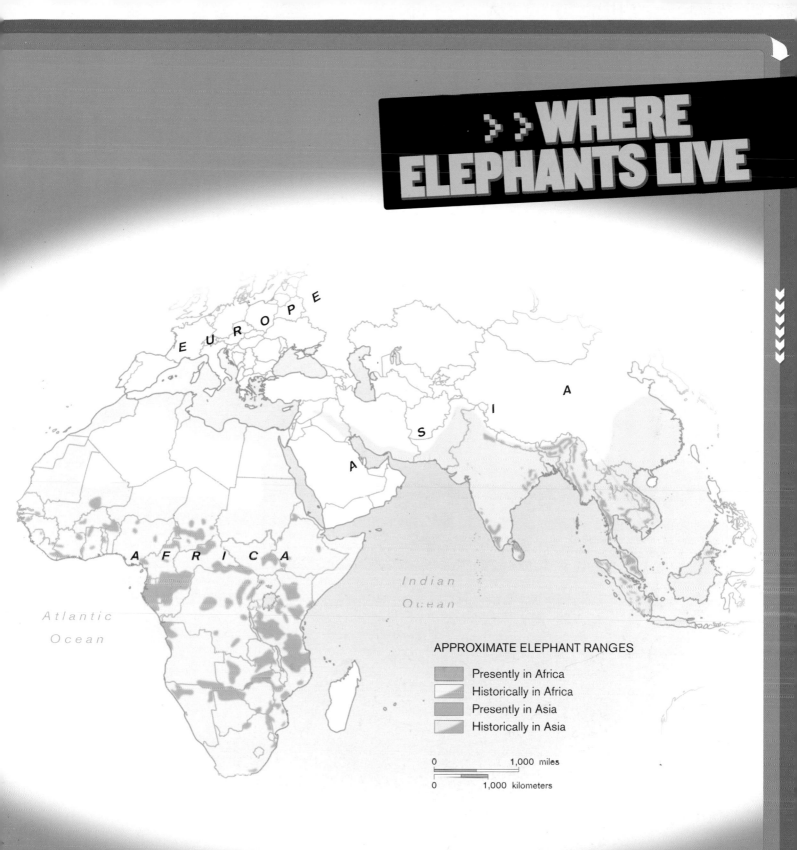

EUROPE

ASIA

AFRICA

Atlantic Ocean

Indian Ocean

APPROXIMATE ELEPHANT RANGES

Presently in Africa
Historically in Africa
Presently in Asia
Historically in Asia

0   1,000 miles
0   1,000 kilometers

>> MEET AN ELEPHANT

BAHATI, THE DESERT ELEPHANT

Bahati belongs to one of the most unique elephant populations in Africa: the desert elephants of Mali. There, fewer than 400 elephants live on the southern edge of the Sahara, where they face extreme temperatures, blinding sandstorms, and a dwindling supply of food and water. To cope in this harsh environment, the elephants constantly move from one water hole to the next. The ancient pathways they follow are critical to the elephants' survival, and Bahati is doing her part to help conserve them.

As part of a scientific study, researchers fitted Bahati and eight other elephants with GPS collars that tracked their movements across the landscape. Traditionally, the Mali desert elephants have enjoyed a peaceful relationship with the local pastoralists who live alongside them, but as more people move into the area, the elephants' pathways become disrupted. The information provided from Bahati's GPS collar is being used to study how humans and elephants can continue to live peacefully together while preserving the elephants' habitat. If all goes according to plan, Africa's most northerly population of elephants will be free to continue roaming their sandy habitat as they have for thousands of years.

ELEPHANTS CANNOT RUN, BUT THEY CAN "SPEED WALK" AS FAST AS 25 MILES AN HOUR (40 KM/H).

A groggy Bahati stands for the first time after being tranquilized so scientists could attach her new GPS collar.

human—with one kick of her pillar-like legs. An elephant is not an animal you would want for an enemy.

In addition to their hulking bodies, two physical traits set these giants apart from other animals: their tusks and their trunks. Tusks are actually extra-long incisor teeth. Elephants use them as tools to peel bark from trees and to dig up roots to eat and water to drink. Tusks also become powerful weapons that elephants use to fight enemies.

An elephant's trunk, also called a proboscis, is a fusion of the animal's nose and upper lip. An adult elephant's trunk stretches to about seven feet (2 m) long and can weigh nearly 300 pounds (136 kg)! That might sound like an inconvenient load to carry, but an elephant's trunk is its most valuable tool. In addition to the essential task of breathing, elephants use their

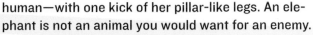

Three Maasai morani use the EleApp to collect data on elephants.

>> ANIMAL RESCUE!

YOU BE THE SCIENTIST

Do you dream of being a scientist? Now you can be! In 2011, elephant scientists Joyce Poole and her partner, Petter Granli, launched a cool new high-tech project through their organization ElephantVoices. Their goal is to build a community of people who care about elephants by connecting people to elephants living in the Masai Mara in Kenya. By using the Mara EleApp, which can be downloaded to a smartphone, anyone can help collect scientific data on the Mara elephants.

The idea is simple: People use their cell phones to snap photos of elephants they encounter and record what they see—like the number of elephants present, if they're a family or an all-male group, what they're doing, and whether any are injured. The phone captures the date, location, and time. Then people can sign in to the ElephantVoices website to help identify the elephants in their photos. The data helps Joyce and her team understand the habitat needs of the elephants and alerts them to potential threats. So far, more than 1,100 Mara elephants have been identified through the EleApp. The project has been so successful that Joyce and Petter have expanded it to a new location: Gorongosa National Park in Mozambique.

But you don't have to visit Africa to participate. Anyone can log in to the website and follow the Mara elephants—and for a fee you can even name one. The money helps support the project and educational outreach.

Check out ElephantVoices at
www.elephantvoices.org.

trunks the way humans use their arms or hands. They pluck grass and leaves to eat, suck up water to pour into their mouths, lift heavy loads, scratch itches, and even hug their friends and family members. Elephants also use their trunks to communicate with each other and to find out important information about their environment.

MEGA-HERBIVORES

Elephants are herbivores, which means they feed on plants. Elephants eat grasses, vines, leaves, roots, twigs, tree bark, and fruit. They use their feet, trunk, tusks, and mouth in delicate coordination, and they use special techniques to find and eat different types of food. For example, they push trees over with their powerful bodies, split the heart of palm (a favorite snack) with their tusks, and grind fruit, branches, and leaves over their large, flat teeth.

It takes a lot of food to fill a giant-size stomach. Adult elephants eat about 300 pounds (136 kg) or more of food a day! It's no wonder elephants spend most of their time eating. To ensure a healthy diet, elephants range over long distances, grazing on grass and browsing on plants as they go. It is because of this trait that elephants play an important role in their ecosystems.

KEYSTONE SPECIES

On savannas, elephants are large gray gardeners. By knocking down trees, they create open spaces in their habitats for grass to grow. Grazing animals like zebras, antelopes, and buffalo eat this grass. If elephants disappeared from the savannas, there would be no other large animals to create this important food source. This situation occurred in the 1970s in Uganda's Queen Elizabeth National Park, where elephant populations plummeted from about 4,000 to a couple hundred. Wooded areas and thickets sprang up throughout the park, choking out the grass. With no more grass to eat, grazers like giant forest hogs and antelopes disappeared from the area.

In forests, elephants play a slightly different role. When elephants knock down trees, they create pathways that other animals like gorillas and sitatungas (a type of small antelope) use to navigate through the forest to find food. Also, when elephants eat fruit found in forests, the large, tough seeds soften inside their stomachs. They poop out the seeds, and other

ANIMAL SUPERPOWERS

POWER SNIFFERS

AN ELEPHANT'S LONG NOSE CAN SMELL WATER MANY MILES AWAY.

WITH ONE BIG WHIFF, AN ELEPHANT CAN DETERMINE WHETHER AN ANIMAL OR HUMAN IS A FRIEND OR FOE.

WARY ELEPHANTS WILL TURN AWAY FROM HUMANS IF THEY KNOW THEY POSE A THREAT.

ELEPHANT EARS HAVE UNIQUE VEIN PATTERNS THAT CAN BE SEEN BY THE NAKED EYE. LIKE HUMAN FINGERPRINTS, NO TWO ELEPHANT EARS ARE THE SAME.

An African elephant uses its tusks to strip bark from a tree in an exploited forest.

PEOPLE CALL ELEPHANTS PACHYDERMS, WHICH MEANS "THICK-SKINNED."

Elephants create a network of trails and clearings through a thick forest.

animals eat them. The seeds that go uneaten sprout into new trees, and because of special nutrients in the elephants' dung, the seedlings grow more quickly. Without elephants, some important tree species would be unable to reproduce, forever changing the structure of the forests.

Only one species rivals elephants on the enormous impact they have on their habitats: humans.

HUMANS VS. ELEPHANTS

Modern machines make it easy for people to cut down trees and clear large swaths of savannas and forests. As human populations grow and spread across the planet, we clear land to make room for ourselves. This spells trouble for elephants, because they need a lot of land to survive.

(continued on p. 26)

>> ELEPHANT SPOTLIGHT

BRAINY BEASTS

Elephants have been observed making simple tools and using them to deal with pesky situations.

They scratch itches against trees ...

They shape tree branches into flyswatters.

They twist clumps of grass into swabs to clean dirty ear canals.

... and pry ticks from their skin with sticks.

>> EXPLORER INTERVIEW

JOYCE POOLE

BORN: FRANKFURT, GERMANY; GREW UP IN AFRICA; AMERICAN CITIZEN
JOB TITLE: CO-FOUNDER & CO-DIRECTOR, ELEPHANTVOICES
JOB LOCATIONS: IL MASIN AND MASAI MARA, KENYA; GORONGOSA, MOZAMBIQUE; SANDEFJORD, NORWAY
YEARS WORKING WITH ELEPHANTS: 38
MONTHS A YEAR IN THE FIELD: 6

How are you helping to save elephants?
I used to spend all my time in the field studying elephant behavior, collecting data, and writing papers. Since 2002, I have also run a small organization, ElephantVoices, with my husband and colleague, Petter Granli. Our mission is to inspire wonder in the intelligence, complexity, and voices of elephants, and to secure a kinder future for them through research and the sharing of knowledge. This, in essence, is what I do, whether I am in the field, holding lectures, speaking to the media, or sitting in the office on my computer. My work just takes different forms depending on where I am.

Favorite thing about your job?
Being in the presence of elephants and sharing my knowledge about them with others.

Best thing about working in the field?
I just love watching elephants. They are so highly social and so very intelligent and complex that I learn something new from them every day.

Worst thing about working in the field?
Long hours in a hot vehicle can get uncomfortable, and being stranded by a vehicle breakdown can be very frustrating.

How can kids prepare to do your job one day?
To do my job is much more than the pure adventure it may seem to be. You need to study biology, or a similar subject, in high school and college, and have real passion and drive for what you do.

Establishing a relationship with a wild elephant named Vladimir, who permitted me to touch him, and being remembered by him after I2 years. It moved me deeply.

A trio of elephants walks across the savanna. Elephants spend most of the day on the move, traveling to their favorite food sources.

An elephant's home range varies in size from 40 to more than 4,000 square miles (100 to 11,000 km^2). People who settle in elephant ranges create road-blocks for elephants traveling between critical food and water sources. Sometimes conflicts erupt, which can lead to injury and death for both elephants and humans.

Habitat loss is a serious, long-term threat to all elephants, but another, more immediate threat looms over nearly every population left on the planet. Poaching, or the illegal hunting and killing of animals, is a battle elephants have faced for years—but today it is at an all-time high. In the year 1900, it's estimated that millions of elephants ranged across Africa and Asia. Today, only about 400,000 to 500,000 remain on the entire planet. Those numbers may sound high, but if nothing is done to stop poaching, more populations will vanish.

Fortunately, the elephants' call for help is being heard. Many people around the world are fighting to reclaim elephant ranges and protect the giants from hunters and poachers. *You* can help, too. The time is now. We can coexist. Elephants need our help!

An Asian elephant crosses a road that runs through the Gibbon Wildlife Sanctuary in Assam, India.

ELEPHANT CORRIDOR

A SMALL, CAT-SIZE MAMMAL CALLED A HYRAX IS THE ELEPHANTS' CLOSEST LIVING RELATIVE.

A train passes through the Gibbon Wildlife Sanctuary in Assam, India.

>> RESCUE ACTIVITIES

YOU CAN HELP SAVE ELEPHANTS

Elephants need our help. Too many are being poached, forced out of their natural habitats, and mistreated. These animals cannot speak for themselves—and they are too often out of sight and forgotten.

After reading this book you will know more about elephants than the vast majority of people. With this knowledge you have the power to raise awareness about the problems elephants face.

Do this challenge to kick off your campaign to help save the lives and habitats of elephants.

Dear Joyce Poole,

My name is Mary and I love elephants. I think the work you do to help save elephants is wonderful. To say thank you I have been telling people about your important work and asked them to help me celebrate it by showing their support and adding their names below. Thank you for helping all those elephants!

Mary See

Names:
Mary See
Saphire Jameson
Phillip Jones

MAKE

GET SUPPORT BY MAKING A PETITION.

A PETITION IS A PERSUASIVE LETTER TO SOMEONE WHO HAS THE POWER TO CHANGE SOMETHING. Petitions are usually signed by lots of people to show that the letter has a high level of support.

YOU COULD WRITE A LETTER TO SOMEONE LIKE THE LEADER OR AMBASSADOR OF A COUNTRY, A LOCAL POLITICIAN, OR A BUSINESS LEADER. Explain the problems elephants face, but also try to suggest some solutions.

ALTERNATIVELY, WRITE A LETTER TO AN ANIMAL RESCUER TO GIVE THEM YOUR POSITIVE SUPPORT. They will certainly appreciate your message.

ACT

COLLECT AS MANY SIGNATURES AS YOU CAN.

ASK AS MANY PEOPLE AS POSSIBLE TO SIGN YOUR PETITION. The more signatures you collect, the more support behind your cause.

GET INTO ONE OR MORE SMALL TEAMS, AND YOU'LL BE ABLE TO COLLECT FAR MORE SIGNATURES. Think of a busy

SEND YOUR PETITION!

ONCE YOU HAVE COLLECTED YOUR LIST OF NAMES, IT'S TIME TO DELIVER YOUR PETITION. Email is the quickest and cheapest way to do this, but there are more effective ways to get noticed.

TRY TO DELIVER YOUR PETITION BY HAND. You will probably need to set up a meeting to do this, which requires more time and patience, but it will be far more effective. You will get the chance to talk to the people it is aimed at in person.

DON'T SEND JUST ONE LETTER. Send LOTS of letters until you get noticed. You could send one every day or a bunch all at once. Or you could send letters to lots of different people to arrive on the same day. Think big and your message is more likely to get through.

Use these tips to make the most of your petition:

1 When collecting signatures, do something dramatic, like carry a sign or make a bold fashion statement, to get more attention.

2 Join a petition that someone else has already started. You will be able to achieve even more together.

3 Consider raising money as you collect signatures. Collecting donations for an elephant charity could directly help rescue missions around the world.

public place where you could stand and ask people to stop and hear what you have to say about elephants. If they agree with your mission, ask them to add their signature.

PUT YOUR PETITION ONLINE AND IT COULD GO VIRAL! In some countries you can directly petition the government. If you get enough support, they will issue you a response or even debate the issue.

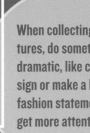

CHAPTER 2

>> LAND OF ELEPHANTS

A herd of elephants stops to drink from a water hole in the Okavango Delta in Botswana.

"ELEPHANTS ARE LIKE PEOPLE, WITH DIFFERENT PERSONALITIES."

—T. N. C. VIDYA, JAWAHARLAL NEHRU CENTRE FOR ADVANCED SCIENTIFIC RESEARCH

Sixty million years ago, a small mammal called *Eritherium azzouzorum* roamed across northern Africa. The mammal looked more like an oversize rabbit than a modern-day elephant, but it turns out *Eritherium* is the elephants' oldest ancestor.

ELEPHANTS TODAY

Over the next several million years, *Eritherium*'s body multiplied in size. Its short snout extended into a long, flexible trunk.

And sleek, dagger-like tusks sprouted from its face, until eventually *Eritherium* evolved into the titanic gray mammals we call elephants today.

Elephants' massive bodies—including long, pillar-like legs and thick footpads that absorb their massive weight—are designed to travel over rough terrain for long distances. Early elephants from the genus *Loxodonta* blazed trails through central Africa's moist tropical forests. As the planet warmed, some groups traveled outside the forests and to the continent's new savannas. These elephants became *Loxodonta africana*, or savanna elephants. Those that remained in the forest became *Loxodonta cyclotis*, or forest elephants.

AN ELEPHANT'S HEART WEIGHS AS MUCH AS 46 POUNDS (21 KG), ABOUT AS MUCH AS A FOUR-YEAR-OLD KID.

THE ELEPHANT FAMILY TREE

The ancestors of the elephant have roamed the earth for millions of years. As science progresses, archaeologists may continue to unearth ancestors that lived more than 60 million years ago.

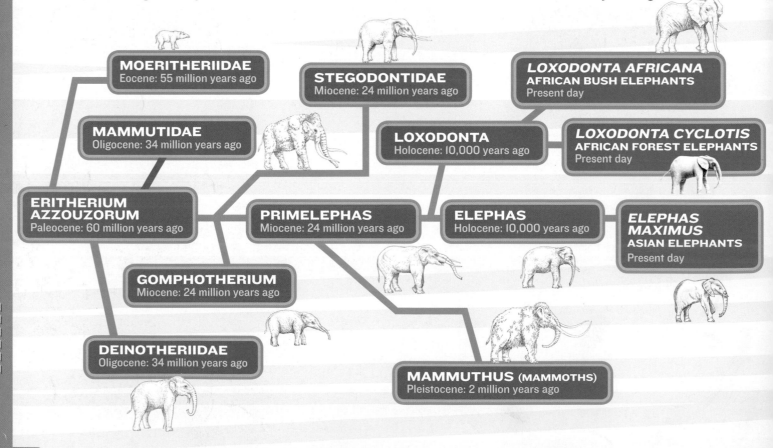

MOERITHERIIDAE
Eocene: 55 million years ago

STEGODONTIDAE
Miocene: 24 million years ago

LOXODONTA AFRICANA
AFRICAN BUSH ELEPHANTS
Present day

MAMMUTIDAE
Oligocene: 34 million years ago

LOXODONTA
Holocene: 10,000 years ago

LOXODONTA CYCLOTIS
AFRICAN FOREST ELEPHANTS
Present day

ERITHERIUM AZZOUZORUM
Paleocene: 60 million years ago

PRIMELEPHAS
Miocene: 24 million years ago

ELEPHAS
Holocene: 10,000 years ago

ELEPHAS MAXIMUS
ASIAN ELEPHANTS
Present day

GOMPHOTHERIUM
Miocene: 24 million years ago

DEINOTHERIIDAE
Oligocene: 34 million years ago

MAMMUTHUS (MAMMOTHS)
Pleistocene: 2 million years ago

ELEPHANT HARDWARE

Millions of years of evolution have hardened elephants for their environment.

An elephant's teeth are like grinding stones that help it break down tree branches and bark.

The skin on an elephant's back, head, and feet can be more than one inch (2.5 cm) thick.

Thick pads on the bottom of an elephant's feet help it keep balance on uneven ground.

An elephant's powerful trunk contains about 150,000 muscle units and no bones—it's the perfect tool for multiple tasks.

An elephant has a built-in cooling system—when it flaps its ears, the skin and blood vessels release heat.

GETTING SMART ABOUT SAVING ELEPHANTS

Poachers have made a habit of invading the thick, tangled forests of central Africa, killing more than half of the elephants in only ten years. They are armed and very dangerous, and park rangers risk their lives every day to thwart poachers' plans. With so much ground to cover over rugged terrain, it is difficult to keep up. That's why conservation scientist Emma Stokes helped develop the Spatial Monitoring and Report Tool (SMART).

SMART is a cutting-edge software program that allows rangers to record and map what they see in the field in real time using handheld computers. Once back at park headquarters, managers use the maps to deploy new teams to the highest-threat areas first. The aim of SMART is to stop the illegal killing of elephants, and it's working.

SMART originally launched in 20 countries, including Gabon and the Democratic Republic of the Congo in Africa. Now Emma and her partners plan to launch SMART in several other countries across Africa and Asia, and they have no plans to slow down. The team is constantly refining the software, and soon rangers will be able to relay the information they collect to park headquarters at the tap of a button, allowing managers to provide even swifter action to save elephants in their range.

A worker carries a pair of tusks that will be sold to the highest bidder at an auction. These tusks will probably be carved into statues or jewelry for people to buy.

Meanwhile, another elephant species, from the genus *Elephas,* had been wandering the continent's drier regions. At some point, though, *Elephas* packed its bags and migrated out of Africa to Europe and Asia. Scientists are not sure what prompted the species to leave, but *Elephas* thrived in its new home range and eventually gave rise to modern Asian elephants, or *Elephas maximus.*

AFRICAN ELEPHANTS

African savanna elephants are the largest surviving elephant species. On average they stand about three feet (1 m) taller than their forest-dwelling cousins. The open habitats where savanna elephants live allowed them to evolve massive bodies. They also sport larger ears than forest elephants. Their big ears help keep them cool under the blistering equatorial sun.

Savanna and forest elephants thrived across the whole of Africa for millions of years, but once humans started hunting them for their ivory tusks, large populations began to vanish. Ivory has played an important cultural role in people's lives for thousands of years. Archaeologists have uncovered 5,000-year-old ivory carving centers from the ancient city of Babylon. Egyptian and Assyrian kings also killed elephants for their tusks. People carved the tusks into statues, jewelry, and other objects and kept them as symbols of wealth. Centuries later, European empires set up

Elephants tower over the land in Samburu National Reserve in Kenya.

THE LONGEST
AFRICAN
ELEPHANT TUSK
EVER RECORDED
MEASURED
10.7 FEET
(3.3 M).

Some of the last big elephant tuskers gather in Tsavo East National Park in Kenya.

special colonies in Africa to harvest elephant ivory and then used the money they earned to finance explorations across the globe.

As the demand for ivory grew, entire elephant populations began to disappear. Elephants vanished from much of their range, and they became extinct in the north of the continent. In the 1950s, national parks were set up to protect elephants, but people around the world still wanted to buy hand-carved ivory. By 1979, the African elephant population had plummeted from tens of millions to just over one million. There wasn't enough ivory from elephants who had died a natural death to meet demand, so criminals began illegally killing elephants and selling their tusks. In ten years, poachers cut the already dwindling African elephant population in half. Only about 600,000 remained.

Finally, in 1989, the Convention on International Trade in Endangered Species of Wild Fauna and Flora (CITES) banned the international trade in ivory. Demand for ivory products fell, and many elephant populations began to recover. Things were looking up for the elephants—until recently. A new wave of

>> MEET AN ELEPHANT
SUDU ALIYA, THE WHITE ELEPHANT

Sudu Aliya is a very special elephant. She's considered a *white* elephant, even though she isn't exactly white. White elephants' skin varies from light gray to pink in color, and they are very rare. Researchers first spotted Sudu Aliya as a baby in 1993 in Yala National Park in Sri Lanka. She is the first—and so far only—white elephant recorded on the island. But Sudu Aliya is special for another reason. She may be the only *wild* white elephant on Earth.

White elephants are an important symbol in the Buddhist religion. People believe the animals are sacred. In the past, people in Asia captured white elephants from the wild and gave them as gifts to powerful rulers. In Myanmar, people once decorated white elephants with jewelry made of gold, rubles, and emeralds. They fed the elephants grass from gold vessels. In Burma, palace performers danced and sang for white elephants. In Thailand today they are considered royal and become property of the king. But Sudu Aliya is lucky—while most white elephants live in captivity, she roams free, protected from outsiders by the dense trees that make up Yala National Park.

A rescued Asian elephant eats sugar cane.

ASIAN VS. AFRICAN ELEPHANTS

Asian elephants and African savanna elephants belong to the same family, but genetically they are as different as lions and tigers. Check out some of the unique physical features that set these two species apart.

Asian elephants have pink patches or spots on their faces, ears, and chests.

Asian elephants have two bulges or domes on their heads, whereas African elephants have only one.

demand for ivory is threatening the giants once more. Poachers are back on the ground, and this time they have organized into large-scale criminal networks that kill around 30,000 elephants every year.

Today Africa's remaining elephants live on patchy pieces of land in four regions: West, East, central, and southern Africa. West Africa and central Africa, where the majority of Africa's forest elephants live, have been hit hardest by poaching. More than half of the forest elephants have been wiped out in the past ten years. East Africa, which was once home to the largest African elephant population, now holds about 110,000. A wave of poaching from 1960 to 1990 claimed more than 90 percent of the region's elephants, and the current poaching is decimating some of Africa's most iconic populations.

Southern Africa is now home to about half of the continent's elephants. While most elephant populations there are fairly secure, with some even growing, poachers loom on the horizon, threatening the last great strongholds of Africa's giants.

ASIAN ELEPHANTS

From a distance, African and Asian elephants may look similar, but side by side there is no confusing them. Asian elephants are slightly smaller with more body hair and have two round domes on their heads, whereas African elephants have only one. Asian elephants' ears are significantly smaller, and they have smoother skin. Perhaps the most important difference between the two types is that not all Asian elephants bear tusks—only the occasional male will have them,

Most Asian elephants are tuskless, whereas the majority of African savanna elephants sport long, heavy tusks.

Asian elephants' ears are much smaller than their African cousins' ears.

and females never do. For this reason, Asian elephants have escaped much of the poaching crisis.

The single biggest threat to Asian elephants is land loss. Asia has one of the fastest-growing and densest human populations in the world. In the past 50 years, many states with elephant ranges have built roads, railway lines, dams, canals, pipelines, and mines, which are disruptive to natural habitats. Crops have also taken over elephant homelands. In Malaysia and Indonesia, oil palm, rubber tree, and sugar cane fields dominate the landscape. In India, there are tea and coffee plantations. Asia is simply running out of space for its giants.

The majority of Asia's 30,000 to 50,000 elephants live in India, which is also home to more than one *billion* people. Humans and elephants live side by side, and they don't always make the best neighbors. Elephants sneak outside their protected areas at night to

ASIAN ELEPHANTS ARE MORE CLOSELY RELATED TO THE EXTINCT WOOLLY MAMMOTH THAN TO AFRICAN ELEPHANTS.

Rainwater pools in man-made trenches in Maharashtra, India.

ELEPHANTS ARE RELATED TO SEA-DWELLING DUGONGS AND MANATEES BUT NOT ELEPHANT SEALS.

An Asian elephant stands chained in a field in India. Privately owned elephants often spend hours chained to one spot when not working.

feast on farmers' crops, causing millions of dollars in damage. Roving elephants also trample around 400 people every year.

The battle for space in Asia is complicated, and more elephants will likely disappear, but there is still time to expand and connect protected areas for the few stable elephant populations. Many people are working to safeguard the elephants' human neighbors and to give Asian elephants a chance to carry on living in the wild.

EXPERT TIPS

Conservation scientist Emma Stokes's tips for studying forest elephants:

1 A good field scientist always carries a notebook and pen to write down things of interest and relevance.

2 Keep your eyes and ears open. Elephants can hide themselves very well—it's possible to walk right past one in the forest if you're not paying attention!

3 Elephants are difficult to observe in thick forests, so scientists often construct wooden platforms in trees near forest clearings to view them. It's important to build the platform downwind of elephants, so they are not disturbed by your scent.

ANIMAL RESCUE!

KEEPING TABS ON ELEPHANTS

To save elephants, you have to know them. And that takes a lot of time, energy, and patience. Just ask field researcher T. N. C. Vidya, who works for the Jawaharlal Nehru Centre for Advanced Scientific Research in Bangalore, India. She also spends time in a forest in southern India getting to know elephants. How exactly does she do that?

Vidya sleeps at a field camp near the forest. She rises before 6 a.m. and drives over bumpy game roads searching for elephants. When she spots one, she identifies it by special markings on its ears, face, or body. Then she settles in to watch the elephant and make notes in her book. She records where it goes and what it does. She even collects poop samples, which she analyzes later to determine if elephants are related. When the sun goes down, Vidya heads back to the field station to enter her data into a computer. Keeping tabs on elephants is a tough job, but somebody has to do it, and Vidya would not have it any other way. She shares the data she collects with wildlife park managers to develop new conservation strategies.

LOOK OUT FOR ELEPHANTS

Explorers, conservationists, geographers, and other experts who look out for elephants spend much of their time watching them. Explorers look to see where elephants are, conservationists may observe how they behave, and many geographers map where elephants come and go. By working together, experts are best able to understand how to save elephants and their habitats.

For this rescue challenge, take the time to watch, observe, and understand elephants. Then make images that help people understand the problems elephants face.

MAKE

CREATE A LOOKOUT POST.

GRAB A CAMERA, FIELD NOTEBOOK, AND A SNACK, AND HEAD TO THE BEST PLACE TO OBSERVE ELEPHANTS IN YOUR LOCAL AREA. Take what you need to get comfy and spend lots of time watching what elephants get up to.

IF YOU ARE LUCKY ENOUGH TO LIVE NEAR A WILDLIFE PARK, SANCTUARY, OR WILD ELEPHANTS, make sure you position yourself in a safe place with a good view.

NOWHERE NEAR ELEPHANTS? Build a den at home and get cozy while watching an elephant series on your TV, laptop, or tablet. This is also a great way to watch and learn about elephants.

ACT

BE ACTIVE BY TAKING PHOTOS OR DRAWING.

CLOSE TO REAL ELEPHANTS? Use your camera to photograph them. Be creative and take unusual pictures that will grab people's attention. Try different effects with your camera, such as a low or high angle, making the elephant look tiny, or a close-up of a single body part, like a tusk or eye.

1 Print stickers that you can wear and pass around at school.

2 Design an elephant mask from a photo or drawing. Print lots of them and ask as many people as you can to suddenly start wearing them at the same time.

3 Design a computer screen saver and share it with your friends and family. Ask your school to use the screen saver on all the computers in the building. You might even be able to persuade your local movie theater to put it on before films.

SHARE

PUT ON A PHOTO SHOW.

Put on a photo show that raises awareness about elephants and how people can get involved. You could:

PRINT YOUR PICTURES AND PUT THEM ON DISPLAY. Make them big to get more attention. Ask permission to display your pictures at a public library, park, or your school.

PUT THEM ONLINE. If you are old enough, share your photos on a social networking site, blog, or other website. Ask people who view your photos to "like" or share them with other people in their networks.

DO SOMETHING UNEXPECTED. Project your photos onto a large wall for all to see when it is dark outside. You will need a projector and the help of an adult.

WATCHING ON TV? Get creative and draw pictures or paintings. Don't worry about trying to make your artwork look precise. Just giving your impression of the elephants can be highly effective. You could even paint them wild colors.

GIVE EACH PIECE OF YOUR ARTWORK A NAME AND A CAPTION. You can use these to help your audience understand some of the problems elephants face.

CHAPTER 3

>> ELEPHANT FAMILY

"ONE JUST HAS TO LOOK AT AN ELEPHANT GROUP TO UNDERSTAND THE IMPORTANCE OF FAMILY."

—DAME DAPHNE SHELDRICK, THE DAVID SHELDRICK WILDLIFE TRUST

An elephant calf finds shelter amid its mother's legs.

t is dusk on the savanna. *PHURRR! PHURRR!* Trumpets blast. A female elephant has just given birth to a baby boy. Other family members circle around the new mother. She wraps her long trunk around the gray bundle lying on the ground and lifts the baby to his feet. He takes his first wobbly steps. *PHURRR! PHURRR!* The family broadcasts their excitement into the night.

FAMILY FIRST

Elephants know how to party, and a newborn elephant is something to celebrate. Elephants are born into tight-knit families composed of related adult females—mothers, daughters, sisters, aunts, and cousins—and their young calves. An elephant herd can number from two individuals to more than 50, depending on where they live. But no matter how big the family, a newborn calf is always the center of attention.

Raising a successful calf takes teamwork. Elephant babies have a lot to learn. Just like human children, they learn by watching and mimicking their mothers and older family members—a process that can take many years.

While elephants are the largest land animals, they still face daily challenges that threaten their survival. Elephant ranges are like dangerous obstacle courses for a young calf just learning to use its legs. Slippery mud, large boulders, and rugged terrain make it tough for a young calf to keep up with the rest of the family, but a long, well-placed trunk by a mother or aunt helps guide it along.

Other obstacles, like gushing rivers, steep banks, and wells, pose bigger threats. In some areas, humans that live in and around elephant habitats dig wells

AN AFRICAN SAVANNA ELEPHANT'S EARS CAN BE AS BIG AS FOUR FEET (1.2 M) ACROSS AND SIX FEET (2 M) TALL!

A mother elephant keeps close watch over her calf as darkness falls. At night, young calves are most vulnerable against predators like lions and tigers.

Wildlife conservationist Hammer Simwinga's tips for studying elephants:

1 Read books based on field research. Some of the books I have enjoyed are those written by Mark and Delia Owens.

2 Take a field trip to elephants' natural habitats, if possible, to understand where and how wild elephants live.

3 Find an experienced and seasoned elephant guide to go with you.

A young African elephant calf tests out its trunk at the Masai Mara National Reserve in Kenya.

ELEPHANT SPOTLIGHT

Elephants have evolved a complex language of sounds and gestures to communicate with one another. Here are just a few:

"I want to play."
Elephants shake their heads from side to side or kneel down, extending an invitation to play.

"Heads up!"
Elephants lift their trunks into the air like a submarine periscope when they detect a new scent and want to alert others to pay attention.

to find water. These wells can litter the landscape like land mines on a battlefield. Once a baby falls in, the family must work together to lift or dig the baby out.

Young elephants spend a lot of time exploring their surroundings. They sniff rocks and bushes, and they chase animals, like birds, monkeys, and buffalo. Calves that stray too far from the group make an easy target for predators such as lions and tigers. If a predator lurks nearby, the adult females bunch together to form a protective wall of towering legs around the young calves, forcing the predators to move on in search of another meal.

Besides navigating tricky terrain and steering clear of powerful predators, newborn elephants have a lot to learn about, well, being an elephant.

ELEPHANT IN TRAINING

For the first two years of life, elephant calves depend on their mothers' milk to survive. After about two or three months, they begin testing solid food. Young calves swipe food out of other family members' mouths—it is how they learn which plants to eat.

Before an elephant can feed itself, it has to learn to master its trunk. A baby elephant is born with no muscle tone in its trunk, which makes it look more like a floppy garden hose than a useful limb. Babies must build strength through practice. It's frustrating at first. Some youngsters cheat and kneel down to bite grass or drink water with their mouths, but after a few months, they begin using their trunks with ease. They fling dust onto their backs in the hot sun and even throw sticks and rocks at their cousins.

"Don't mess with me."
An aggressive elephant will spread its ears wide and hold its head high to tell another animal it means business.

"Let's go!"
A matriarch points her body in one direction, lifts her front leg, and lets out a rumble to tell the group to get moving.

Young elephants love to play. They splash through water holes and push each other around. If their roughhousing gets out of hand, an aunt or older sister will step in to separate them for an elephant time-out.

ALLOMOTHERS

The act of caring for another family member's calf is called allomothering. Allomothering is like babysitting. Female elephants begin caring for younger calves when they are around four or five years old. Not only is allomothering critical to a calf's survival, but it is also a way for young females to build important skills to be a good mother.

Allomothering comes naturally to a young female elephant, but it will be several more years before she is ready to be a full-time mother. Female elephants typically have their first baby when they are about 14 or 15 years old. An elephant's first baby is the trickiest, but she can rest assured that her own mother, sisters, aunts, and cousins will be there to lend a helping hand—because females stay with their family groups for life.

THE GOVERNMENT OF BOTSWANA RECENTLY PASSED A LAW BANNING THE HUNTING OF ELEPHANTS—AND ALL OTHER ANIMALS—IN THE COUNTRY.

THE LONG GOODBYE

While young females are helping to care for babies, the males are busy playing with other males their age. Unlike some animals, elephants are not territorial and their ranges overlap. An elephant family can cross paths with 100 or more elephants in a single day. Some elephant families keep to themselves, while others form lasting friendships. Young males spend much of their time wrestling and sparring with young males from other families. Rambunctious males are not just horsing around, though. Play fighting is important for their development. The skills they learn will come in handy later in life, when the males begin competing for mates. Over the next few years, the young males spend more and more time away from their families, and by the age of about 14 they leave them for good.

ANIMAL SUPERPOWERS

SUPER SENSORS

WHETHER AN ELEPHANT BLASTS A HIGH-PITCHED TRUMPET SOUND OR A LOW RUMBLE, A COPY OF THE SOUND VIBRATES THROUGH THE GROUND.

FAR-OFF ELEPHANTS SENSE THE VIBRATIONS IN THEIR FEET.

THEY FREEZE AND ASSESS THE SITUATION.

THEN THEY ACT.

THE ELEPHANT MAY HEAD TOWARD THE VIBRATIONS,

OR HIGHTAIL IT OUT OF THERE!

TARRA, DOG'S BEST FRIEND

Most of the elephants that live at the Elephant Sanctuary in the U.S. state of Tennessee pair up with another elephant buddy and become best friends. Not Tarra. She preferred a much smaller, hairier companion: a stray canine named Bella.

Bella followed Tarra all over the sanctuary grounds. Together they strolled through the woods, swam in the pond, and lounged in the sunny pasture. Bella snuggled close to Tarra at nap time. And Tarra stroked Bella's back with her massive elephant foot, as if she were petting the dog. Then one day Bella got injured. Her back legs stopped working, and she was taken to the office above the elephant barn to recover—but that didn't stop Tarra from seeing her furry friend. Every day for three weeks, the elephant visited her companion at the office. Soon, Bella recovered and the two pals returned to their old routine roving the sanctuary, proving that dogs are more than just man's best friend.

Two young male forest elephants spar in the water. Forest elephants' tusks, which are shorter and straighter than their savanna-dwelling cousins', are often pink or brown in color.

BABY ELEPHANTS SUCK ON THEIR TRUNKS THE WAY HUMAN BABIES SUCK ON THEIR THUMBS.

Adult males typically spend time in all-male bachelor groups. Group living has its advantages for adult males, too. Older males offer protection from predators, but more important, they act as role models for young males. Teenage males tail older males like a shadow, watching their every move. If an adult sniffs a urine spot on the ground, the young male wanders over and takes a whiff, too. Young males also watch how the older males interact with females, and with time they adopt their more gentlemanly behavior.

As male elephants age, their hormones kick in. When they are about 30 years old, male elephants begin to enter periods called musth. During musth, they become aggressive. The males leave a trail of urine, and glands on their temples swell and leak fluid. It is their body's way of telling them it's time to look for a mate.

(continued on p. 58)

A mother elephant stops to allow her calf a drink of milk.

BHASKAR CHOUDHURY, BVSC

BORN: ASSAM, INDIA
JOB TITLE: REGIONAL HEAD (ASSAM) AND HEAD VETERINARIAN, WILDLIFE TRUST OF INDIA AND INTERNATIONAL FUND FOR ANIMAL WELFARE
JOB LOCATION: NORTHEAST INDIA
YEARS WORKING WITH ELEPHANTS: 13
MONTHS A YEAR IN THE FIELD: 9-10

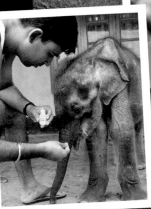

How are you helping to save elephants?
I am part of a team who helps elephants in crisis and distress. We mostly handle Asian elephant calves after they get separated from the natal herd due to man-made and natural reasons. We try to reunite such calves with their herd, but if we fail to do so they are brought to a rehabilitation center for nursing and care. After four or five years, they are relocated to a natural habitat for rehabilitation into the wild. We also treat injured juvenile and adult elephants for injuries.

Favorite thing about your job?
The challenge that each case of animal rescue presents and how we work together as a team to overcome this. Every day and every hour is another pleasure that no other profession can provide. I really enjoy this workplace of mine.

Best thing about working in the field?
You have a stress-free life. Life in the field is simple, and you stay young and energetic every day. The fresh air and magnificent sceneries help!

Worst thing about working in the field?
Nothing, except that you are cut off from the rest of the world for most days. When you go to the town or city you need a little time to adjust to the noises there.

How can kids prepare to do your job one day?
Only those who have a genuine interest should take up this job. Ability to sacrifice is another important factor to be successful in this field. Frustration will take over if interest and sacrifice is not there.

We have successfully rehabilitated ten Asian elephant calves back to the wild after they were rescued at a very young age. Each one is memorable. We have not only saved their lives but also helped them to enjoy their life in the wild with their counterparts.

Just like their African cousins, Asian elephants gather at water holes to drink and socialize.

ELEPHANT EMERGENCY!

On September 9, 2000, wildlife veterinarian Bhaskar Choudhury received a frantic call from forest guards in Kaziranga National Park in India.

A newborn elephant calf was tangled in water hyacinth, a floating plant, in a river. "Come quick!" they told him. Bhaskar rushed to the scene. Luckily, some local elephant handlers had managed to pull the struggling elephant from the river. Bhaskar examined the infant. It was free of injury, but frightened.

Bhaskar works for the Wildlife Trust of India. He and his colleagues help rescue and rehabilitate elephant calves that get separated from their families. In this case, the torn-up riverbanks indicated that the herd had attempted to save the calf but failed and eventually moved on. But that day, the scared little elephant was lucky.

A large herd was sighted about half a mile (1 km) from the river. Bhaskar and his team escorted the tiny elephant through nine-foot (3-m)-tall grasslands to a swampy clearing. There, the infant saw its family and cried out. The entire herd circled around the calf, rumbling reassurance and welcoming him home. To Bhaskar, nothing is more rewarding than seeing an elephant he helped save living a normal life in the wild.

When a bull comes into musth, he begins the search for females. If two musth males of the same size meet, they may fight. On one occasion in Amboseli National Park in Kenya, two musth males approached each other. The giants stared each other down and circled like boxers in a ring. Then the elephants lunged, launching heavy blows with their heads and tusks. After ten grueling hours, the slightly smaller male backed off, exhausted from the fight. The victorious bull had established his dominance.

When elephants finish mating, the female's family blasts their trumpets and roars their approval. The only celebration that rivals a newborn elephant's birth is after a female has mated. Perhaps the family is already anticipating the arrival of the next baby. Nearly two years later they will gather once again to welcome their newest family member into the world.

A newborn Asian elephant calf stands in tall grass. The calf is about the same age as the one Bhaskar helped rescue and reunite with its family.

STAYING COOL

Elephants have developed some creative ways to stay cool in their hot habitats.

They splash through water holes and wallow in mud.

They use their trunks to spray water over their bodies. Then they sprinkle a layer of dust or sand on themselves to create a thick paste, or "elephant sunscreen."

They store water in a special pouch in their throats. When it is hot they insert their trunks into this pouch, withdraw water, and spray themselves.

Young calves cool off by taking cover in the shadows cast by their mothers' legs.

>> RESCUE ACTIVITIES

EXPLORE LIKE AN ELEPHANT

Elephants are threatened not only by poachers, but also by habitat loss. They can be active for up to 20 hours and travel 30 miles (48 km) or more a day searching for food, water, and mates. With forests and grasslands being turned into farmlands and cities, it is increasingly difficult for elephants to get around.

By doing this challenge, you will get a feel for what it might be like to be an elephant for a day. You will also get lots of opportunities to talk to people about how to save elephants from extinction.

MAKE

DRESS LIKE AN ELEPHANT.
DESIGN AND MAKE YOURSELF AN AWESOME ELEPHANT COSTUME. Start by tying on an elephant-style tail. Some rope should do it.

CREATE LIFE-SIZE ELEPHANT EARS. This is very easy to do with large sheets of paper or poster board. You could even attach them to a headband or hat.

MAKE YOURSELF A TRUNK AND TUSKS. A large piece of flexible plastic will make a good trunk. Using a hose, you could even make it squirt water. Tusks can easily be cut from a large cardboard box. You will need to work as a team of two, deciding who will hold up the tusks and who will control the trunk.

ACT

EXPLORE LIKE AN ELEPHANT.
PUT ON YOUR COSTUME AND SPEND A DAY BEHAVING LIKE AN ELEPHANT. If possible, get a large group together to form a family. Roam your habitat looking for food and water.

KEEP IT REAL BY BEING ACTIVE FOR TEN HOURS. Remember, elephants are active for up to 20 hours a day! Make sure you set aside time to play. Elephants love to wallow in water holes.

EAT ONLY FRUIT, LEAVES, AND PLANTS FOR THE DAY. You can avoid poisonous plants by buying your food from a grocery store. Elephants eat as many as 100 different plants in a given area. Could you nibble on 50?

SHARE

LET PEOPLE KNOW ABOUT YOUR ELEPHANT JOURNEY.

SHARE YOUR EXPERIENCE by using your elephant adventure to talk to people about the problems that elephants face.

WHEN PEOPLE GIVE YOU STRANGE LOOKS, say hello and explain to them what you are doing.

GET EVEN MORE STRANGE LOOKS. Send pictures of your "herd" to your local newspaper. Try to go viral online. Take a video of an elephant trombone tune and accompany it with a dance routine.

>> EXPERT TIPS

Don't by shy! Use these tips to get some serious attention on your elephant adventure:

1 Make some noise! If possible, carry a trombone in your parade and use it to communicate with each other, especially when you are out-raged at something. A loud keyboard, trumpet, or other instrument could work as well.

2 If someone gives you a hard time, push your ears for-ward to make yourself look as big as possible. Step your front legs onto a log or tree stump to appear taller.

3 Feeling hot? Take a mud bath or blow water down a hose pipe onto your back. You can also go for a swim using a snorkel the way an elephant uses its trunk.

CHAPTER 4

> > > ON THE MARCH

"ELEPHANTS LEAD A VERY LOVELY SOCIAL LIFE. THEY'RE NEVER MORE THAN ABOUT FIVE YARDS [4.6 M] FROM ANOTHER ELEPHANT."

—CYNTHIA MOSS, DIRECTOR OF THE AMBOSELI TRUST FOR ELEPHANTS

A family of African elephants takes time out on the savanna to eat and socialize.

Lightning crackles in the distance and thunder booms. Dark gray storm clouds loom high above the dry savanna. On the ground, long lines of elephants march in from every direction. They are right on time. Small raindrops quickly transform into a downpour. The wet season has arrived.

AN ELEPHANT NEVER FORGETS

Getting drenched in the rain might sound annoying to humans, but to elephants water is life. Rain means lush green grass and flowering fruits will soon follow. Every year, most elephant families—led by an intrepid matriarch—walk many miles in their annual migrations following the rains.

A family's matriarch—typically the oldest and largest female in the group—tells the family what to do and where to go, especially when food sources dry up. Unlike some animal leaders, the matriarch does not win her role through fighting or a show of dominance. She is the wisest.

Elephants have excellent memories. A matriarch passes the knowledge she has learned over many years down to younger family members. She remembers important things like the locations of the best water holes, how to avoid predators, and the annual migration route. This critical knowledge was passed down to her from the previous matriarch.

The older the matriarch, the better. "A family led by an old matriarch benefits from her experience and wisdom. They are role models to other families, they survive droughts best, and they are able to raise the most babies," says Joyce Poole, a biologist who has studied elephants for decades. A good matriarch is a family's key to survival.

THE AVERAGE ADULT ELEPHANT'S BRAIN WEIGHS ABOUT TEN POUNDS (4.5 KG)— MORE THAN THREE TIMES THE SIZE OF A HUMAN BRAIN.

ELEPHANTS SLEEP LYING DOWN FOR ONLY A COUPLE OF HOURS EACH NIGHT.

A group of African elephants huddles together and waits out the rain in the Samburu National Reserve in Kenya.

A wise and gentle Echo dines on grass in Amboseli National Park.

ECHO, ELEPHANT SUPERSTAR

Echo is probably Africa's most famous elephant. She is the star of several films and books. Researchers met the intrepid matriarch in Amboseli National Park in Kenya in 1973 and followed her for nearly 40 years. During that time, Echo's family grew from 7 individuals to 40—twice as many as any other elephant family in Amboseli! This rough-and-tumble matriarch proved her strength as a mother and a leader time and time again on the unforgiving savanna.

Echo gave birth to at least eight babies over the years. One son, named Ely, was born unable to straighten his legs. The newborn calf shuffled along on his knees for three straight days, but Echo stuck by his side nudging him forward. Finally, he gained the strength to walk like the rest of his family. Years later, a dominant elephant family kidnapped Echo's young calf Ebony. In an epic show of strength and bravery, Echo gathered the largest females in her family, charged toward the bullies, and rescued the tiny elephant.

Echo's leadership extended beyond her own babies. Echo led her family to food and water during two horrible droughts. The year she passed away, 400 elephants died in a drought, but remembering the ancient routes their wise leader had taught them, Echo's family survived.

ELEPHANTS MAY EAT MORE THAN 100 DIFFERENT TYPES OF PLANTS IN ANY GIVEN AREA.

GREAT MIGRATION

Elephants were born to move. Wild elephants spend at least 20 hours a day on the move—eating, exploring, or socializing—but nothing tests an elephant's body like their annual migration. The desert elephants of Gourma, Mali, trek 300 miles (483 km) through the rugged, sweltering Sahel Desert in northern Africa every year. It is the longest elephant migration on Earth—and the hottest. Temperatures can soar above 120°F Fahrenheit (49°C), but the elephants march on. They must reach the next oasis to survive.

Not all elephants migrate. Some forest elephants have easy access to year-round food and water, but they may trek many miles to gather at their favorite feeding grounds at different times of the year. In the Central African Republic, more than 100 forest elephants gather at a swampy clearing called Dzanga bai to eat, drink, and dig for mineral salts locked inside the mud. Salt is an important part of an elephant's diet that they cannot always get by eating their usual array of plants.

Some elephants go to great lengths in search of salt. In Loango National Park In Gabon, scientists believe elephants ingest salt by foraging on saltwater-soaked vegetation that grows along the coastal beaches that line the forest. Miles away in Kenya, elephants that live near an extinct volcano trek into deep underground salt mines to get their fix. They scrape salt from the cave walls and dig it up from the floor. Salt-hungry elephants actually formed many of the caves that dot the landscape in this area over thousands of years.

Food and minerals are not the only items on an elephant's seasonal agenda. The wet season marks the biggest social event on an elephant's calendar. Elephant gatherings are like big family reunions.

ELEPHANT SOCIAL NETWORKS

Elephants enjoy being around other elephants, and their social networks are huge. If elephants were on Facebook, they would likely have hundreds of friends. Even in the dry season, nonrelated elephants regularly cross paths, but during the wet season, hundreds and sometimes thousands of elephants converge onto a single area.

>> ANIMAL RESCUE!

CURBING CONFLICT IN INDIA

>>>

The Western Ghats mountain range in southwestern India is considered one of the planet's "hottest hot spots" of biodiversity. The Ghats are currently home to nearly 100 globally threatened animal species, including the world's largest population of Asian elephants. Conservation scientist Krithi Karanth aims to keep it that way, but that is no easy task in a country where humans and elephants are in a constant battle over space. Krithi's philosophy: start with the people.

Krithi launched an ambitious research project to get to the bottom of human-wildlife conflict in India. In the Indian state of Karnataka, her team interviewed people living in over 1,300 villages surrounding protected areas in the Western Ghats.

It turned out that elephants and wild pigs were the top two culprits in raids on farmers' crops. Using this data, Krithi's team created a map of the most vulnerable areas so that park managers could focus conservation resources there first. Krithi's team also helps farmers report crop-raiding incidents to the government so they can get paid for the damages, helping to keep the offending elephants safe from retaliation.

>> ELEPHANT SPOTLIGHT
LIVING WITH ELEPHANTS

The wells elephants dig provide water for other animals that share their habitat—even humans.

Living with elephants has its advantages. You could think of them as the big brothers and sisters of the animal kingdom.

Dung beetles roll bits of elephant poop into balls, which they stow underground to eat later.

Two or more related families that regularly socialize together are called bond groups. Elephants in bond groups help protect one another and care for one another's young. Bond groups may include anywhere from one to five families. Elephants in bond groups greet one another with excitement. They rumble loudly and tangle their trunks in a type of elephant hug.

However, not all elephants are friendly. Like humans, elephants have unique personalities and can sometimes be bullies. These elephants will chase others away from an area to keep it for themselves. Some have even been known to display their dominance by kidnapping babies from other families!

To guard against bullies, wise matriarchs can recognize the voices of more than 100 different elephants, and they have learned over the years which families to avoid.

WET AND DRY SEASONS

The wet season is a time of plenty. Elephants gorge themselves on their favorite grasses, fruits, and leaves. Even the adults hang out with their friends and play. Elephants are excellent swimmers—they will plunge their entire bodies deep underwater, then shoot to the top and breach, or rise out of the water, and flop on their sides like a whale.

Elephants create forest clearings and keep them free of trees so that grass can grow.

White birds called cattle egrets hitch rides on elephants' backs.

Ogooué Leketi Elephant Project director
Inkamba Nkulu Clement's tips
for tracking forest elephants:

1 Learn as much as you can about elephant behavior before going into the field.

2 When tracking forest elephants, keep a distance of at least 25 feet (7.5 m). Never approach an elephant from behind or from the side.

3 Be sure to set up your camp away from elephant trails, or you could get trampled!

Like all good things, the wet season eventually comes to an end. The rains stop and the savanna dries out. With the time of plenty coming to an end, the elephants say goodbye to their friends and head separate ways, just as they came.

Dry-season home ranges center around the last remaining water holes in an area. Several bond groups and families may share the same dry-season home range. Those that do are called a clan. They typically move in smaller groups, walking from place to place to find food and waiting for the rain to fall again. But what happens if the rain doesn't come?

Droughts—long periods of two or three years with little or no rainfall—are relatively common in savanna ecosystems. This is when a wise old matriarch proves her worth. In 1992, a severe two-year drought devastated Tarangire National Park in Tanzania. Food sources in the park dried up, and elephants had to act

ELEPHANTS USE THEIR TRUNKS AS SNORKELS WHEN THEY WADE INTO DEEP WATER.

Snorkel up! A young elephant swims across the Chobe River in Botswana using its trunk as a snorkel.

Beverly and Dereck Joubert photograph an elephant at *very* close range in Botswana.

intelligently or risk death. It had been 34 years since the last drought swept through the park, and only the older matriarchs would have experienced it. Those brave matriarchs knew what to do and led their families out of the park to other food sources they had remembered from their youth. Unfortunately, the families with younger matriarchs stayed put and experienced twice as many deaths as those that left.

Eventually, though, storm clouds gather once again, and rain advances across the horizon. Matriarchs gather their families, and everyone falls in line for the long journey back to their wet-season habitats.

>> ANIMAL RESCUE!

FILMING GIANTS

National Geographic explorers-in-residence Dereck and Beverly Joubert have been filming and photographing elephants in the wilds of Botswana for 30 years. Their goal is to give viewers around the world a glimpse into wild elephants' lives so that they can appreciate the animals even if they've never met them.

Hanging out with elephants can be a dangerous job. Dereck and Beverly creep along the savanna in a large truck. They try to keep silent and make themselves invisible so they can capture images of elephants behaving naturally. On one expedition, the jeep made a creaking sound that startled a large female. Before Dereck and Beverly could blink, the elephant rammed her head into their truck, rolling it backward down the path at top speed. Dereck hit the brakes just in time to avoid falling into a deep hole. Annoyed that she could no longer bully the truck, the elephant lunged at the vehicle one last time, then flapped her ears and turned away. It was a close call, but to Dereck and Beverly it was a small price to pay to share space with these amazing animals in their natural habitat.

>> RESCUE ACTIVITIES

SUPERSIZE YOUR CAMPAIGN

Elephants are one of the largest and most famous species of animal on the planet. If you explore a few shops and keep your eyes open, you may be surprised by the number of elephants that you will see. They appear on flags and company logos, as toys, and in films, cartoons, and books like this one.

We all know them for their large bodies, incredible trunks, and pointy tusks. But what if they did not have any tusks? Would anyone notice? Do this challenge to find out.

MAKE

STEP UP YOUR CAMPAIGNING.

CHOOSE A CAMPAIGN NAME. This could be Mission: Elephant Rescue (the name of this book) or something that you have thought of yourself.

DESIGN A LOGO TO HELP PEOPLE RECOGNIZE YOUR CAMPAIGN. You could write a slogan. This is a short sentence that summarizes your aim, like "Saving Elephants Together."

KEYWORDS OR HASHTAGS ARE A USEFUL WAY TO FOLLOW HOW SUCCESSFUL YOUR CHALLENGES HAVE BEEN. Ask your supporters to include #YourCampaignName when they comment or share photos.

ACT

CREATE A NOTICEABLY LARGE HERD OF TUSKLESS AFRICAN ELEPHANTS.

TAKE ACTION AND PUT YOUR ELEPHANTS ON DISPLAY.

FIRST, PICK A LOCATION. It should be somewhere that many people will see it, but you want to be sheltered from wind and rain, too. You don't want your elephants to fly off!

MAKE SURE YOU INCLUDE A SIGN OR DISPLAY THAT EXPLAINS WHAT YOU ARE DOING AND WHY. You could explain the number of elephants that are killed for their tusks each day, month, or year.

DO THEY NOTICE THAT THE ELEPHANTS DO NOT HAVE TUSKS? Use this question as an opportunity to start a conversation about the problems elephants face. Encourage your supporters to take photographs of your elephants and share them on the Internet. Give them a caption that they could include when sharing their pictures. Always ask a parent or guardian before going online.

INVITE LOTS OF PEOPLE TO HELP YOU SUPERSIZE YOUR CAMPAIGN. Plan what you are going to do in advance. Make sure you have all the materials you need and jobs that everyone can do.

BE HEARD WITH A MASSIVE HERD! Make lots and lots and lots of tiny elephants out of paper. The more you make, the more you will be noticed. Remember not to give them tusks.

BUILD THE BIGGEST ELEPHANT THAT YOU POSSIBLY CAN from sheets, boxes, and anything else you can get your hands on. If you make a whole family, you will get even more attention!

Making lots of tiny elephants is easier than making a big one and could have a much bigger impact. You could:

1 Make hundreds of elephants and put them all in one noticeable place.

2 Display them in lots of different places in your school, so that wherever they go, people see them.

3 Be careful not to litter. This could send out the wrong message and you could end up getting into trouble instead of praised.

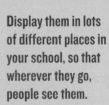

CHAPTER 5

>> ELEPHANTS AND PEOPLE

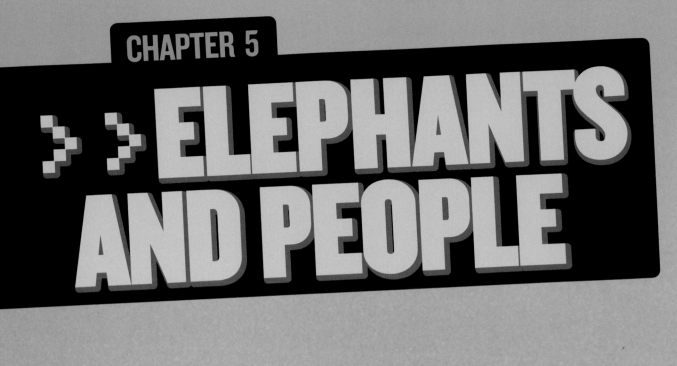

"I BELIEVE PEOPLE WILL ONLY PROTECT WHAT THEY LOVE, AND THEY WILL ONLY LOVE WHAT THEY UNDERSTAND."

—JOYCE POOLE, ELEPHANT SCIENTIST AND CONSERVATIONIST

Tourists in a safari jeep get a close-up look at African elephants in Kenya.

Long before army tanks and fighter jets carried soldiers into war, men rode elephants into battle. Ancient Indian texts tell us it looked something like a wall of giants marching toward enemy lines. Metal armor protected the elephants' heads and sides. A mahout, or elephant trainer, and three soldiers rode atop each giant's back. The soldiers drew their arrows and shot at their targets on the ground.

ELEPHANT WARS

Well-trained war elephants made fearsome opponents. They attacked forts and trampled horses and people. Mahouts trained their elephants to hold the enemy down with their feet and impale them with their tusks. The elephants could also snatch men from the battlefield with their trunks and deliver them up to the mahout. The tactic of deploying war elephants became so popular it eventually spread from India to northern Africa and across the Mediterranean Sea to Greece.

Some western rulers bought trained war elephants from Indians in the east, while others captured and trained African elephants. Egyptian ruler Ptolemy II captured elephants from the upper Nile River region to

A painting depicts Alexander the Great battling an Indian army and its war elephants.

ELEPHANT HEROES

Some cultures revere elephants so much that they consider them sacred and worship them as gods.

In India, Hindus pray to the elephant-headed god Ganesh before starting something new.

White elephants are considered sacred to Buddhists.

Some African tribes wear elephant masks in ceremonies, which scientists believe represents a spiritual connection to the animal.

In Laos and Thailand, Hindu people revere a three-headed elephant, Erawan. Each head represents one of the three main Hindu gods—Brahma, Vishnu, and Shiva.

COUNTING FOREST ELEPHANTS

Counting elephants in the thick forests of central Africa is tricky, but it is important for forest managers to plan effective conservation and anti-poaching projects. Luckily, Inkamba Nkulu Clement, director of the Ogooué Leketi Elephant Project, is up for the challenge. He treks through the sweltering central African forests following elephant trails and looking for evidence of the giants.

Forest elephants like to gather in swampy clearings called bais, so Clement installs motion-sensitive video cameras to help him record and identify individual elephants that visit the clearings. The problem is that bais also attract poachers, making Clement's work dangerous. On one excursion, three poachers armed with machine guns entered the bai where he and his team were working. Clement hit the record button on his camera as one of his teammates approached the men. He told the poachers they were there to study elephants but that unfortunately they had not seen any signs of elephants there for three days. The poachers retreated, but Clement thought fast. He immediately called authorities from his satellite phone to report the poachers, and his video helped authorities nab the culprits.

Forest elephants walk into Dzanga bai, a popular meeting spot for elephants and other animals in Dzanga-Ndoki National Park in the Central African Republic.

An elephant adorns a tile made in Pakistan in 2000 B.C.

stock his elephant corps. Farther west, Carthaginians loaded elephants onto ships and sailed across the Mediterranean Sea. They marched the towering titans into battle against the Romans.

King Pyrrhus of the ancient Greek state of Epirus deployed elephants in battle against the Romans, too. At the Battle of Heraclea in 280 B.C., his elephants panicked the Roman horses, making them run off. King Pyrrhus claimed victory. People continued to train and deploy war elephants for thousands of years.

ANCIENT ART

Long before humans conquered elephants, they feared and even revered them. Rock art from the Sahara reveals unique clues to one ancient human-elephant relationship. Thousands of years ago the region was a vast savanna, not a desert. Rivers and acacia trees were scattered across the landscape as they are in East Africa today. Millions of animals roamed the land, including elephants.

Written text had not been invented. Instead, people painted and carved images into rock. Many millions of carvings can still be seen today on the large rocky plateaus that stick up out of the sand, like pages from an old history book. Many of the carvings show humans herding cattle, sheep, and goats. Some even show humans milking cattle, which tells us that the humans who created the images likely had a dominant relationship with these animals and depended on them to survive.

The elephant carvings, however, show a different picture. Many of these images show the gray giants towering over tiny humans. Elephants were not really that big, so why did people draw them that way? Researchers think the images could mean that the people who drew them saw elephants as massive and majestic animals. One carving shows an elephant prancing along looking joyful, as if during a greeting ceremony, according to elephant expert Joyce Poole. Others show humans cowering in fear beneath the

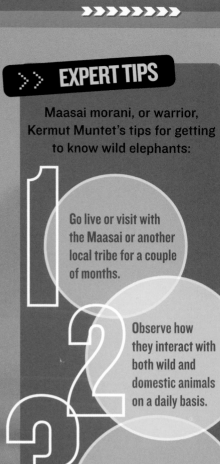

Maasai morani, or warrior, Kermut Muntet's tips for getting to know wild elephants:

1 Go live or visit with the Maasai or another local tribe for a couple of months.

2 Observe how they interact with both wild and domestic animals on a daily basis.

3 Remember wild animals are wild. Keep your distance, especially if you see an elephant with a calf.

A young Maasai family tends their herd of goats.

A Maasai morani, or warrior, keeps close watch over a family of elephants in the Masai Mara in Kenya.

giants. We cannot know exactly how the people who drew these images felt, but researchers believe they were likely in awe of elephants. They saw elephants as dominant and dangerous—beasts to fear for sure—but they also admired them.

ELEPHANT TRAILS

Some African cultures learned to depend on elephants to survive. The Maasai and Samburu people of Africa live southeast of the Sahara in the countries of Kenya and Tanzania. Both belong to a traditional nomadic morani, or warrior, culture that dates back thousands of years. They build simple mud huts and raise cattle, sheep, and goats in the savanna.

Traditionally, when the rains stopped and the grass dried up, Maasai and Samburu families packed up their things and moved to greener pastures. They built new huts and settled into their homes for the next three to four years. How did they know where to go? They followed the elephants. "Elephants are kind of like the masterminds of nature. They know where the food and water are," says Nickson Kiong'a, who grew up in a Samburu village in northern Kenya. Without the elephants' guidance, their livestock would not survive.

(continued on p. 86)

ANCIENT SYRIANS HUNTED ELEPHANTS TO EXTINCTION IN THEIR REGION MORE THAN 2,000 YEARS AGO.

83

>> EXPLORER INTERVIEW

INKAMBA NKULU CLEMENT

BORN: BRAZZAVILLE, REPUBLIC OF THE CONGO
JOB TITLE: DIRECTOR, OGOOUÉ LEKETI ELEPHANT PROJECT
JOB LOCATION: REPUBLIC OF THE CONGO
YEARS WORKING WITH ELEPHANTS: 15
MONTHS A YEAR IN THE FIELD: 8

How are you helping to save elephants?

I run a biological inventory in an area not surveyed before, where local people and poachers confirmed that elephants are present. I also created three teams: a patrol team to survey the area every month to keep out poachers, a semipermanent team based in forest clearings to monitor the area where elephants regularly gather, and a monitoring team to survey elephants in all the protected areas.

Favorite thing about your job?

I love forest elephants for the simple fact that they are beautiful, good, noble, and inspiring examples of wild nature. For an ecologist, working in the field by following elephant paths is like having a window opened. Suddenly the forest becomes alive with signs of elephants that would otherwise be invisible.

Best thing about working in the field?

There is nothing quite like walking silently through the deep forest on a huge old elephant trail watching out for the scarred trees, the browsed leaves, the lines of elephant footprints, and the warm fresh dung full of seeds that will help create the next 1,000 years of tree cover.

Worst thing about working in the field?

Working in the forest can be dangerous, especially if you are not paying attention.

How can kids prepare to do your job one day?

Working with elephants in the field demands courage and the knowledge of how to approach these mammals. Learn about elephant behavior in advance, and prepare the appropriate equipment in town before deploying into the field.

MEMORABLE MOMENT

>>

While studying elephant feeding behavior ten years ago, I accidentally startled an adult female elephant with my camera flash. She charged at me, and I didn't understand how I left the place alive. I wanted to quit after that, but my supervisor encouraged me to keep going. I'm glad I did.

An African forest elephant herd marches through Odzala National Park in the Republic of the Congo.

Today, the Samburu and Maasai people still depend on elephants. Their villages are now permanent, but when droughts strike, men still gather their livestock and follow the elephants, while women and children stay back in the villages. "The elephants are the guides," Kiong'a says.

A SHOW OF POWER

Humans' ancient relationship with elephants must have been one of awe and even fear, but somewhere along the line, this relationship changed. The Indus Valley civilization was probably the first to capture wild elephants and put them to work. People trained Asian elephants to haul heavy loads, to pull logs out of forests, and eventually to fight as war elephants.

Elephants became part of everyday life in these societies. People put elephants on display in major cities, much as people put animals in zoos today. Wealthy men and women owned and rode elephants for pleasure, and people hunted elephants for sport and for ivory. Remnants of these ancient practices can still be seen throughout the world today.

ELEPHANTS AND PEOPLE TODAY

About one quarter of Asia's elephants today are captive. Most of them are privately owned and rented out by mahouts to work in logging or construction, or they are painted, decorated, and paraded in religious festivals and ceremonies. The ancient practice of being a mahout is passed down through family tradition from father to son. Children as young as seven learn to ride the elephants and control them through a series of hand and foot signals and verbal commands. It will become their profession and the only way they know how to make a living.

However, these ancient practices are dangerous and controversial. Elephants are wild animals and they must first be trained to follow directions. In a brutal technique called fear-based training, many mahouts tie down the elephants with ropes or chains and beat them until they obey. Sometimes the elephants act out, trampling their mahouts and other people who come to watch the festivals.

In addition to capturing elephants to be put to work in Asia, many African and Asian countries still ship wild elephants overseas to circuses and zoos that may

ELEPHANTS HELPED HAUL AND HOIST HEAVY STONE AND MARBLE SLABS INTO PLACE TO BUILD CAMBODIA'S FAMOUS ANGKOR WAT TEMPLE IN THE 12TH AND 13TH CENTURIES.

Mahouts command these working elephants in Thailand to pull logs from a forest.

SAVING ELEPHANTS IN THAILAND

When Lek Chailert was 16 years old, she visited a logging camp in a forest in northern Thailand near where she grew up. She witnessed elephants being forced to work with no breaks until they collapsed. Some were even beaten by their owners. That was the day Lek decided she would dedicate her life to saving elephants.

Several years later, Lek built Elephant Nature Park (ENP) just outside of Chiang Mai, Thailand. She trekked through forests and scoured city streets looking for working elephants to rescue. On one trip, Lek met an elephant named Medo. The elephant had a broken hip but was still forced to pull logs up a steep hill for logging trucks to collect. The elephant cried out in pain. For five months, Lek worked to convince Medo's owner to let her rescue the injured elephant. Finally, her persistence paid off and she brought Medo to live with her in the sprawling natural habitat at ENP.

Lek has rescued more than 200 elephants like Medo, but she doesn't stop there. Lek educates other people on why it is important to protect these majestic animals and their habitats. Her goal is to secure a brighter future for all of Thailand's elephants.

use similar fear-based training methods. Fortunately, some efforts are being made to change these methods in zoos to a system of reward-based training—where an elephant is given food for following instructions— and to create bigger and better living environments. And some countries have enacted laws against the capture and export of baby elephants due to the trauma it causes them.

The biggest threat to wild elephants' lives is still land loss and the human greed for ivory. Today the illegal ivory market is three times larger than it was before the 1998 ban, with the largest demand coming from China and the United States. It is estimated that one elephant is killed every 15 minutes for its ivory. What's worse is that this "blood ivory" is funding other illegal activities, including terrorist groups. Fortunately, many people around the world are working hard to stop ivory poachers and to change the human-elephant relationship back to one based on respect before it is too late.

>> RESCUE ACTIVITIES

TELL AN ELEPHANT'S STORY

"**A**n elephant never forgets" is a well-known saying that has its roots in an elephant's ability to remember ancient routes for finding food, water, and safety. We humans are excellent at remembering things, too.

Stories are a powerful way to communicate the challenges that elephants face and can be easier for people to remember than dry facts. By reading the story of a specific elephant, people are more likely to understand and remember the issues that you tell them about. By doing this challenge, you will develop a story you can use to help your campaign.

MAKE

PLAN AN ELEPHANT STORY.

DECIDE WHAT YOUR MESSAGE WILL BE. What do you want your readers to learn by reading your story? Do you want them to learn about poaching, habitat loss, an elephant conservation success story? Or something else?

FIND YOUR STORY. You could make up a story, retell one from this book, or research a true story yourself.

PICK YOUR FORMAT. You could create an illustrated children's book, a poem, song, or play, or even a set of instructions.

ACT

A CIRCUS ELEPHANT
ONE Day there lived a baby Elephant called 'Dumbo' HE Loved to do alot of acts.

Dumbo was trained to do acts, Dumbo had gotten beaten to do these cool acts. which made them feel really sad.

And then got forced to do the acts.

TELL YOUR STORY.

LET PEOPLE READ THE STORY FOR THEMSELVES. Print copies to be given to friends or stocked in your library. You could email a copy to your local newspaper or publish it yourself online.

SHARE YOUR STORY AS A PERFORMANCE. This could be as simple as a public reading or as elaborate as a full theatrical play.

AT THE END OF YOUR STORY, YOU COULD ASK YOUR AUDIENCE TO CONTRIBUTE TO YOUR CAMPAIGN. They could sign a petition, help you raise funds, or help spread awareness for elephants.

GET SOME ATTENTION FOR YOUR CAMPAIGN.

DO SOMETHING EXTRAORDINARY. Create a massive story by writing just three sentences in huge letters on an enormous piece of paper.

PROVIDE A PICTURE OF AN ELEPHANT AND ASK LOTS OF PEOPLE TO WRITE SHORT STORIES ABOUT IT. Display all of the stories on a wall, including yours, so that everyone can read them.

PROBLEMS FACED BY ELEPHANTS ARE HIDDEN TO MOST OF US. We are just too far away to see them. Write your story in invisible ink that can be seen only with a special light. Ask people to read your story using the light and you will give them a more memorable experience.

Struggling to decide what your story should be about? Here are some tips that will help you:

1 Write something based on a true story. Researching a story based on real events might make it easier to write about, and your audience may connect with it more.

2 You could write from the point of view of an elephant or someone who spends his or her life protecting elephants.

3 Keep it short. People sometimes lose interest during long stories, and you wouldn't want them to miss your message!

CHAPTER 6

>> SAVING ELEPHANTS

"DESPITE FAILURES, WHEN SUCCESS COMES YOU REALIZE THAT YOUR EFFORTS HAVE SAVED A WILD ELEPHANT."

—BHASKAR CHOUDHURY, WILDLIFE VETERINARIAN AND ELEPHANT RESCUER

A family of African elephants weave through a dense, soggy marsh in Amboseli National Park in Kenya.

Saving elephants takes teamwork. Their ranges often stretch beyond park boundaries, cross borders between countries, or are so remote that it is difficult for authorities to keep an eye on elephants. Luckily, a movement to protect mega-landscapes in Africa and Asia is gathering steam.

TEAMWORK IN TANZANIA AND KENYA

The borderlands between southern Kenya and northern Tanzania comprise a vast area that stretches more than 435 miles (700 km) and spills into both countries. Sixteen protected parks dot the landscape and are home to one of Africa's largest elephant populations. A recent spike in poaching prompted scientists, conservationists, government officials, and local citizens to join forces.

They created a detailed map of the landscape and are now piecing together information about local elephant populations. The goal is to map the animals' movements across the entire region, identify areas with human-elephant conflict, and pinpoint poaching hot spots. The countries will work together to create cross-border conservation strategies. The initiative is a giant leap toward protecting the region's elephants, but it is still in the early stages.

In the meantime, local organizations help fill in the gaps. At Amboseli National Park in Kenya, rangers lacked the equipment and manpower to fight crime. The situation across the border in Tanzania, where some Amboseli elephants travel, was even worse. An organization called Big Life Foundation stepped in to help. They recruited more than 300 local Maasai warriors and trained a new team of rangers to track poachers on both sides of the border. Patrolling more than 2 million acres (80 million ha) of elephant territory is no easy task, but the rangers faced the challenge head-on. In their first two years they arrested more than 600 poachers. It is a success story for the region, but not all countries can afford to patrol vast elephant ranges.

(continued on p. 99)

SOME COUNTRIES HAVE BURNED OR CRUSHED ILLEGAL IVORY CONFISCATED BY AUTHORITIES SO THAT IT CAN NEVER REENTER THE MARKET.

>> ANIMAL RESCUE!

ELEPHANT INVESTIGATOR

Bryan Christy is helping fight for elephants by going behind the scenes and doing some serious—sometimes dangerous—detective work. As a renowned investigative journalist and public speaker, he travels around the world uncovering the secrets of illegal animal smuggling and other environmental crimes. And all of this in-the-field work has put him in some interesting situations. Throughout the years, he has been bitten between the eyes by a blood python, chased by an alligator, and sprayed by a tarantula, all in the service of wildlife.

Christy is especially passionate about exposing elephant poaching methods. In 2012, he wrote an article for *National Geographic* magazine called "Blood Ivory" that detailed the history and practices of illegal ivory smuggling in several countries, a previously untold story.

Besides investigative pieces, Christy engages the public in the fight for elephants in many ways, including speaking at universities and international organizations and inspiring people to educate themselves and talk about the situations elephants face on the blog A Voice for Elephants, of which he is a founding editor.

Named National Geographic's 2014 Explorer of the Year, his extensive work on wildlife crime is included as one of ten ways National Geographic has changed the world and continues to inspire people and lawmakers to take a stand against poaching and other forms of cruelty.

Officials burn 5.5 tons (5 mT) of illegal ivory in Tsavo East National Park in Kenya.

>> EXPLORER INTERVIEW
DAME DAPHNE SHELDRICK

BORN: KENYA
JOB TITLE: FOUNDER, THE DAVID SHELDRICK WILDLIFE TRUST
JOB LOCATION: KENYA
YEARS WORKING WITH ELEPHANTS: 50
MONTHS A YEAR IN THE FIELD: 12

How are you helping to save elephants?
We have rescued, reared, and rehabilitated more than 150 orphaned elephants back into the wild community of Tsavo East National Park. We assist the Kenya Wildlife Service by providing security, fuel, eight fully equipped anti-poaching teams working in conjunction with rangers, and aerial surveillance on a daily basis, and by funding three fully equipped mobile veterinary units to treat the sick and the maimed.

Favorite thing about your job?
The best reward of our work is when an ex-orphaned elephant, now living a normal wild life, brings back its wild-born calf to share with the human family (i.e., the keepers).

Best thing about working in the field?
Being among nature and the natural world. It uplifts the spirit, refreshes the soul, humbles one, and brings one's problems back into perspective.

Worst thing about working in the field?
We have to endure heartbreak over and over again when a dearly loved elephant baby dies in our arms. I think the tears I have shed over elephants could fill a bathtub.

How can kids prepare for your job one day?
An innate love and understanding of the natural world is a must, as is a reverence for life, and understanding that every species belongs to the earth and is necessary for the well-being and balance of the whole. You must do whatever you can to help, save, and care for any animal in need, but most importantly know how to say goodbye when the time comes.

Daphne Sheldrick plays with an orphaned baby elephant at the David Sheldrick Wildlife Trust's elephant orphanage in Nairobi, Kenya.

>> **MEMORABLE MOMENT**

Being within touching distance of a majestic, wild bull elephant with awesome ivory reaching right to the ground. His wild entourage had befriended our ex-orphans now living wild and took the cue from them to accept us as trusted friends.

>> ANIMAL RESCUE!

PROTECTING ELEPHANTS IN ZAMBIA

More than 100,000 elephants once roamed throughout Luangwa Valley in Zambia. Then poachers invaded the area. Local villagers agreed to help the poachers kill elephants for their ivory. At the time, it was the only way they could make money to feed their families, and by 1986 only about 1,000 elephants remained. The giants needed help, and fast. Conservationist Hammer Simwinga grew up in northern Zambia, and he had an idea.

Hammer knew that elephants could provide a different type of income for villagers in the form of eco-tourism. So he formed a nonprofit organization and lent money to local people so they could start their own businesses. People used the money to plant crops, and soon local stores popped up along new "Main Streets." The stores sold the farmers' goods and employed other people as bookkeepers and salesclerks. Because people now had a different way to earn money, poaching in the area plummeted, and today North Luangwa National Park is thriving once again. New safari lodges have sprung up across the landscape, providing even more jobs for people. Hammer has helped transform the lives of more than 35,000 people in 60 villages!

African elephants stop to eat in Gorongosa National Park in Mozambique. To fill their large stomachs, elephants spend most of the day walking and eating.

DNA DETECTIVE

One sleuthing scientist may have found a solution that could help put authorities in Africa and Asia one step ahead of poachers. Biologist Samuel Wasser and his team of researchers at the University of Washington's Center for Conservation Biology collect elephant poop all across Africa. Back in their lab, they extract DNA from the samples and use it to build a continent-wide DNA reference map. Then, when authorities find illegal ivory stashes in Africa, Asia, Europe, North America, or elsewhere, they send the ivory to Sam's lab.

By comparing the DNA in the ivory to his reference map, Sam can often pinpoint exactly where the ivory came from. Over time the map will reveal poaching hot spots and trade routes across the continent, allowing countries, national parks, and nonprofit organizations to focus their efforts on the highest-risk areas first.

ECOTOURISM

Tourists pay money to see elephants, lions, giraffes, and other animals in the wild. This is called ecotourism, and part of the money earned helps protect the animals' habitat. This approach has become so

A hut in Gorongosa National Park in Mozambique

popular that some people in Africa go to great lengths to bring animals back to places that have lost wildlife.

Gorongosa National Park in Mozambique is home to mountainous rain forests, lush wetlands, and grassy savannas. Forty years ago, the park teemed with wildlife. Then a 15-year civil war devastated the country, and soldiers killed animals for food. Poachers thrived in the chaos, and more than 90 percent of the park's large animals vanished. The elephant population shrank from over 4,000 to a mere 150.

A few years later, an American philanthropist teamed up with the government of Mozambique. Together they launched the Gorongosa Restoration Project to restore the park's natural beauty. Park staff trucked in hundreds of buffalo, wildebeests, zebras, and several bull elephants from other game reserves to kick-start the process. They hired local scouts to guide tourists up Mount Gorongosa, and they constructed lodges in the park to entice ecotourists.

Today Gorongosa's animals thrive. The elephant population alone has grown to 350 individuals. The park still has a long way to go to fully recover, but with the support of the Gorongosa Restoration Project, the local people, and ecotourists, the animals once again have a chance.

FIGHTING TO SURVIVE IN ASIA

In Asia, where the human population creeps further into elephant ranges every day, the problem of saving elephants is trickier to solve. Human-elephant conflict is high, and protecting what few habitats exist is crucial. The goal is to develop wildlife corridors, or large stretches of land that connect protected areas so that elephants and other wildlife can travel safely. An organization called the International Fund for Animal Welfare (IFAW) is at the front of this effort. Their first major project is to link two elephant habitats in a northwestern state of India.

Kaziranga National Park in Assam is dominated by low-lying grasslands. Elephants, rhinoceroses, sloth bears, tigers, and hundreds of other animal species live there. The Brahmaputra River, which borders the northern edge of the park, provides lush vegetation and year-round water for the animals. A problem arises during monsoon season when the river gushes with water and floods the plains. Rising water drives the animals out of the park in search of higher and

ANIMAL SUPERPOWERS

SNEAKY BEASTS

ELEPHANTS SHOW THEIR CRAFTY SIDE TO OVERCOME OBSTACLES.

WILD ELEPHANTS NEUTRALIZE ELECTRIC FENCES WITH LOGS, THEN CHARGE THROUGH.

SOME WORKING ELEPHANTS STUFF MUD INTO BELLS THEIR OWNERS FASTEN AROUND THEIR NECKS.

THEN THEY SILENTLY SNEAK INTO NEARBY FARMS TO SNAG TASTY CROPS!

ELEPHANTS HELPING HUMANS

Elephants have been helping humans haul heavy loads for centuries, though today these practices are considered controversial. Many people—including scientists, conservationists, and ordinary citizens—are waging campaigns to abolish these practices.

In Myanmar, mahouts train elephants to pull logs out of steep teak forests. It's hard work even for powerful giants.

Elephants that escaped the deadly Indian Ocean tsunami that struck Southeast Asia in 2004 helped survivors clean up the debris.

Elephants near Jaipur, India, carry tourists along a hillside pathway leading to the 400-year-old Amber Palace.

>> MEET AN ELEPHANT

TINKU, THE ELEPHANT ORPHAN

At two months old, a single accident changed the course of Tinku's life. He was born into an elephant family in Kaziranga National Park in Assam, India, but after wandering into a tea field, he fell into a drainage ditch. He cried out to his family, but they could not help him—the ditch was too deep. All hope seemed lost until the Assam Forest Department arrived at the scene.

A hoard of onlookers gathered as rescue workers dug the infant elephant out of the ditch. At last they freed him! Only now his family was nowhere in sight. The loud machinery the workers used must have scared the elephants back into the forest. Tinku was transported to a nearby wildlife rescue center, where he met other orphaned elephants around his same age. Keepers fed the calves milk from a bottle, and when the orphans were big enough and strong enough, they were trucked to another national park to be released into the wild. Today Tinku roams freely through the forest among other wild elephants.

drier land, where they face a gauntlet of dangerous man-made obstacles. Highways, irrigation ditches, electric fences, and train tracks crisscross this area.

IFAW is working with local villagers to free up and protect a stretch of land that connects the park to a wildlife sanctuary on the other side of the villages. For elephants and other animals, the corridor will make crossing the gauntlet of man-made obstacles a lot safer. The project has been so successful that IFAW is already beginning the process of clearing corridors in other parts of India, too.

WILD ONCE MORE

In many Asian-elephant-range countries, large intact habitats are long gone and human-elephant conflict is on the rise. These situations require a more creative approach. In the communities of Prey Proseth and Trang Troyeng in southwestern Cambodia, homes and farms line the edge of the rain forest. At night, elephants emerge from the forest to eat the farmers' crops, and in the past some farmers shot them to protect their fields. But a concerned conservationist

named Tuy Sereivathana (Vathana for short) had an idea. What if the farmers could safely frighten the elephants away?

Vathana, working for a global conservation organization called Fauna & Flora International, has helped organize a community watch group that takes turns standing guard at night. If an elephant wanders too close to the crops, it hits a trip wire that announces its presence. The guards then spring into action, shooting off fireworks and blaring foghorns that scare the elephants back into the forest without hurting them. In the eight years since the project began, not a single elephant has died due to human-elephant conflict. Now the people not only protect the elephants, they respect them as majestic wild animals once again.

It is clear that saving elephants is much more than a one-person job. Hopefully the enthusiasm behind conflict-free corridors, anti-poaching projects, and crafty human-elephant conflict solutions will continue to spread throughout Africa and Asia, giving all elephant populations a better shot at survival. Are *you* up for the challenge to save the world's elephants?

>> **ANIMAL RESCUE!**

RAISING BABY ELEPHANTS

The David Sheldrick Wildlife Trust's elephant orphanage in Nairobi National Park in Kenya has rescued and rehabilitated more than 150 baby elephants. The organization's founder, Dame Daphne Sheldrick, who was the first person to successfully raise an orphaned African elephant under the age of two, developed a special milk formula to replace their mothers' milk. And she formed a new human family of elephant keepers to replace the elephants' wild ones.

Today—due to high rates of poaching and the loss of adult elephants through conflict with humans—the orphanage is bustling. And raising baby elephants is an around-the-clock job. The keepers feed the elephants milk from a bottle every three hours. They walk them into the bush for a midday mud bath and a game of soccer, and they sleep next to the pachyderms at night. Eventually the orphans transition back to the wild to live with other ex-orphans and a wild herd, but many come back to visit the orphanage. A female named Emily even brought her newborn elephant by to meet her human family—a day that Daphne and the keepers will never forget.

>> RESCUE ACTIVITIES

HOLD A CRIME-SCENE INTERVENTION

Too many elephants are killed without anyone knowing who ended their lives. Poaching elephants for tusks is one of the biggest threats that elephants face. Luckily for some, there are people working around the clock to try and stop the poachers who commit these crimes.

Are you ready to be a CSI rescue challenge activist? An intervention is when you take action to change a situation. The situation we want to change is how elephants are dying at the hands of poachers and how they are losing their habitats. This challenge will shock people, stop them in their tracks, and give you the opportunity to talk to them about your campaign.

MAKE

CREATE A SCENE.

PULL TOGETHER A TEAM. Gather some chalk, a clipboard, and some notes on the number of elephants that are poached each year. Get dressed in something official looking, like suits or lab coats.

SET UP A FICTIONAL CRIME SCENE FOR A POACHED ELEPHANT. First, find a public place. It should have lots of space where many people pass by.

DRAW AN ACCURATE SHAPE OF AN ELEPHANT ON THE GROUND WITH CHALK OR TAPE. This should look like the line around bodies that the police use at the site of murder investigations.

ACT

STOP AND SEARCH

QUESTION WITNESSES WHO WALK BY. Be serious and ask people if they saw suspicious activities in the area. Ask if they have seen anyone carrying tusks.

AFTER YOUR INITIAL QUESTIONS, EXPLAIN WHAT YOU ARE *REALLY* DOING. Describe how elephant poaching is such a problem. Have some photos and facts on hand in case people want more information.

ASK PEOPLE TO SUPPORT YOUR CAMPAIGN by signing your petition, helping you collect funds, or spreading awareness for elephants.

GET YOUR MESSAGE OUT TO MORE PEOPLE.

TELL THE MEDIA ABOUT YOUR EVENT so more people will know about your cause. Before the event, email invitations to your local newspaper, radio station, or TV news channel.

DURING YOUR EVENT, TAKE LOTS OF PHOTOS. You could even make a short video. Ask witnesses who walk by to take a picture of the crime scene and share it online, explaining what it is all about.

AFTER YOUR EVENT: Write an email that includes a short recap of what you did, why you did it, and a few of your best photos. Send it off to newsletters, blogs, newspapers, and to anyone else who you think would be interested in your campaign.

>>> BECOME AN EXPERT

There are many professionals who work directly and indirectly with elephants. By doing well in school, you could work towards these jobs:

VETERINARIAN
Vets have a deep understanding of animal-health issues, medicine, and how to help animals in need. While most work with cats, dogs, or farm animals, some vets work with elephants in zoos and in the wild.

CAMPAIGNER
You could run campaigns to help raise awareness and funds for elephants, just like you have done in this book.

GEOGRAPHER
Geographers research how people, wildlife, and habitats are connected. They help governments and charities make big decisions to help protect elephants.

One day Zongoloni will roam free across the African savanna, like this wild adult elephant.

Months have gone by since Zongoloni was rescued. In a few years, she will join older orphans at one of the David Sheldrick Wildlife Trust's reintegration units in nearby Tsavo East National Park. There she will mingle with ex-orphans and other wild elephant herds. When she is eight to ten years old, Zongoloni will transition to a life outside the orphanage walls.

But even after Zongoloni becomes a wild elephant, her human family will always welcome her back to the orphanage. Ex-orphans return often to visit the keepers and other rescued elephants. Some stop by just to "say hello." Others return if they are injured, knowing they will receive care from the keepers. And still others have families of their own and return to introduce their wild-born calves to their human family. The keepers and staff at the David Sheldrick Wildlife Trust hope to see Zongoloni with a calf of her own some day. Until then, they are happy knowing that her physical and emotional wounds have healed.

A brave and happy-looking Zongoloni stands tall in her new home at the David Sheldrick Wildlife Trust.

>> RESOURCES

WANT TO LEARN MORE?
Check out these great resources to continue your mission to save elephants!

IN PRINT

Downer, Ann. *Elephant Talk: The Surprising Science of Elephant Communication.* Minneapolis, Minnesota: Twenty-First Century Books, 2011.

Joubert, Beverly and Dereck Joubert. *Face To Face With Elephants.* Washington, D.C.: National Geographic Society, 2008.

Kingdon, Jonathan. *Mammals of Africa.* New York: A&C Black, 2013.

O'Connell, Caitlin and Donna M. Jackson. *The Elephant Scientist.* New York: Houghton Mifflin Harcourt Publishing, 2011.

Shoshani, Jeheskel. *Elephants: Majestic Creatures of the Wild.* New York: Checkmark Books, 2000.

Sukumar, Raman. *The Story of Asia's Elephants.* Mumbai: Marg Foundation, 2012.

Van Aarde, Rudi. **"Elephants: A Way Forward."** Cape Town, South Africa: International Fund for Animal Welfare, 2013.

WATCH

An Apology to Elephants. Dir. Amy Schatz. Perfs. Lily Tomlin. HBO Documentary Films, 2013.

Battle for the Elephants. Dir. John Heminway. Prod. Katie Carpenter, John Heminway, and J. J. Kelly. Perfs. Jonathan Davis. PBS, 2013.

Cynthia Moss on Elephant Mothers. International Fund for Animal Welfare. Web video.

Echo: An Elephant to Remember. Dir. Mike Birkhead. Perf. Martin Colbeck and Cynthia Moss. PBS, 2010.

Echo of the Elephants. Prod. Marion Zunz. Perfs. David Attenborough and Cynthia Moss. BBC, 1993.

Elephant Rage. Prod. David Hamlin. National Geographic Channel, 2005.

Elephant Whisperer. Dir. Johann Sigfusson. Prod. Anna Dis Olafsdottir and Johann Sigfusson. Parthenon Entertainment, 2012.

Forest Elephants: Rumbles in the Jungle. Prod. Lucy Meadows. Perf. Richard Armitage. BBC, 2009.

Great Migrations: Feast or Famine. Prod. David Hamlin. Perf. Alec Baldwin. National Geographic Channel, 2010.

Secret Language of Elephants. Online video. CBS News. *60 Minutes,* December 26, 2010.

War Elephants. Dir. David Hamlin. Perf. Bob Poole and Joyce Poole. National Geographic Wild, 2012.

ONLINE

African Conservation Center
Works to conserve the diversity of life for the well-being of all people and the environment
www.conservationafrica.org

Amboseli Trust for Elephants
An organization that works to support the conservation of Africa's elephants
www.elephanttrust.org

Cambodian Elephant Conservation Group
A group dedicated to ensuring the survival of the Asian elephant in Cambodia
http://www.fauna-flora.org/explore/cambodia

Celia's Corner
A campaign to end the ivory trade
www.ecosysaction.org/celia's-corner

Center for Conservation and Research
Promoting environmental conservation through science in Sri Lanka
www.ccrsl.org

Foundation for Wildlife and Habitat Conservation
Conservation organization that works to decrease poaching and improve living conditions for people living in the rural areas of Zambia
www.fwhc.net

Save the Elephants
A group that works to protect elephants and their habitats around the world
www.savetheelephants.org

Wildlife Conservation Society
Working to save wildlife and wild places across the globe
http://www.wcs.org

Wildlife Films Botswana
Promotes wildlife conservation through TV documentaries and films
www.wildlifefilms.co

SELECTED SCIENTIFIC PAPERS

Campos-Arceiz, Ahimsa and Steve Blake. "Megagardeners of the Forest—the Role of Elephants in Seed Dispersal." *Acta Oecologica* 37 (2011): 542–553.

Chiyo et al. "Association Patterns of African Elephants in All-Male Groups: The Role of Age and Genetic Relatedness." *Animal Behavior* 81 (2011): 1093–1099.

Christy, Bryan. "Ivory Worship." *National Geographic* (October 2012).

"Elephants in the Dust: The African Elephant Crisis." United Nations Environmental Program, 2013.

Fortham, Deborah et al. "An Elephant in the Room: The Science and Well-Being of Elephants in Captivity." Tufts Center for Animals and Public Policy, 2009.

Hart, et al. "Large Brains and Cognition: Where Do Elephants Fit In?" *Neuroscience and Biobehavioral Reviews* 32 (2008): 86–98.

Maisels F., Strindberg S., Blake S., Wittemyer G., Hart J., et al. "Devastating Decline of Forest Elephants in Central Africa." *PLoS ONE* 8(3) (2013): e59469. doi:10.1371/journal.pone.0059469

McComb et al. "Leadership in Elephants: The Adaptive Value of Age." *Proceedings of the Royal Society B* (2011): 278, 3270–3276.

Poole, Joyce and Cynthia Moss. "Elephant Sociality and Complexity." In *Elephants and Ethics: Toward a Morality of Coexistence*, edited by Christen Wemmer and Catherine A. Christen, 69–100. Baltimore, Maryland: Johns Hopkins University Press, 2008.

Poole, Joyce and Petter Granli. "Mind and Movement: Meeting the Interest of Elephants." In *An Elephant in the Room* edited by Deborah L. Forthman, Lisa F. Kane, Parcel F. Waldau, Robert P. D. Atkinson, 2–15. North Grafton, Massachusetts: Tufts Center for Animals and Public Policy, 2009.

Siebert, Charles. "Orphans No More." *National Geographic* (September 2011).

Sukumar, Raman. "A Brief Review of the Status, Distribution and Biology of Wild Asian Elephants." Zoological Society of London, 2006.

Turkalo, Andrea K. and J. Michael Fay. "Forest Elephant Behavior and Ecology: Observations From the Dzanga Saline." In *African Rainforest Ecology & Conservation*, edited by William Weber, Lee J. T. White, Amy Vedder, and Lisa Naughton-Treves, 207–213. New Haven, Connecticut: Yale University Press, 2001.

ORGANIZATIONS IN THIS BOOK

Big Life Foundation
For more information, check out page 94.
www.biglife.org

The David Sheldrick Wildlife Trust
For more information, check out pages 12, 96, 103, and 107.
www.sheldrickwildlifetrust.org

Elephant Nature Park
For more information, check out page 89.
www.elephantnaturepark.org

The Elephant Sanctuary
For more information, check out page 53.
www.elephants.com

ElephantVoices
For more information, check out pages 19 and 24.
www.elephantvoices.org

Fauna & Flora International
For more information, check out page 102.
http://www.fauna-flora.org

Gorongosa Restoration Project
For more information, check out pages 19 and 100.
www.gorongosa.org

International Fund for Animal Welfare
For more information, check out pages 100 and 102.
www.ifaw.org/united-states

Jawaharlal Nehru Centre for Advanced Scientific Research
For more information, check out page 43.
www.jncasr.ac.in

Ogooué Leketi Elephant Project
For more information, check out pages 80 and 84.
programs.wcs.org/congo

Performing Animal Welfare Society
For more information, check out page 88.
www.pawsweb.org

University of Washington Center for Conservation Biology
For more information, check out page 99.
www.conservationbiology.uw.edu

Wildlife Trust of India
For more information, check out page 58.
www.wti.org.in

PLACES TO SEE ELEPHANTS AROUND THE WORLD

Amboseli National Park, Kenya
David Sheldrick Wildlife Trust, Kenya
Elephant Nature Park, Chiang Mai Province, Thailand
Gorongosa National Park, Mozambique

Kaziranga National Park, India
Okavango Delta, Botswana
Performing Animals Welfare Society (PAWS), California, U.S.A.

>> INDEX

>> IMAGE CREDITS

PHOTO CREDIT ABBREVIATIONS: GI=Getty Images, IS=iStockphoto, MP=Minden Pictures, NGC=National Geographic Creative, SS=Shutterstock

FRONT COVER: Karl Ammann/GI **BACK COVER:** Denis-Huot/naturepl.com **SPINE:** Lori Epstein/NGC **FRONT MATTER:** I, Beverly Joubert; 2-3, Michael Nichols/NGC; 4-5, Beverly Joubert/NGC; 6 (LE), Marina Cano Trueba/SS; 6 (INSET LO), SecondShot/SS; 6 (UP), Tim Fitzharris; 6 (LO), Karl Ammann/Digital Vision; 7 (LORT), Matthias Breiter/Minden Pictures; 7 (UPRT), Darren Moore; 7 (UPLE), Lisa & Mike Husar; 7 (LOLE), Tim Davis/Corbis; 8-9, Beverly Joubert; 10-11, David Sheldrick Wildlife Trust; 12-13 (ALL), David Sheldrick Wildlife Trust **CHAPTER I:** 14-15, Chris Johns/NGC; 16 (LO), Michael Nichols/NGC; 18-19, Jake Wall; 19 (CTR RT), ElephantVoices; 20, Terry Biddle; 21, Chris Johns/NGC; 22, Michael Nichols/NGC; 23 (CTR LE), David Woodfall/MP; 23 (LOCTR), Richard du Toit/MP/NGC; 23 (UPRT), Ben Horton/NGC; 23 (CTR RT), Diane Levit/Design Pics/GI; 24 (UPRT), ElephantVoices; 24-25, Sergio Pitamitz/NGC; 26 (LOLE), Kevin Schafer/MP; 26-27, Kevin Schafer/MP; 28 (BOTH), Daniel Raven-Ellison; 29 (CTR), Daniel Raven-Ellison; 29 (LORT), Tim Fitzharris **CHAPTER 2:** 30-31, Beverly Joubert/NGC; 32, Gary Hincks /Science Source; 32 (UP CTR) Enno Kleinert/Alamy; 32 (LORT) I76/Corbis; 33 (CTR LE), Nick Garbutt/naturepl.com/NaturePL; 33 (UP CTR), Jason Edwards/NGC; 33 (UPRT), Thomasaurus/IS; 33 (LORT), Michael Nichols/NGC; 33 (LOLE), Jason Edwards/NGC; 34 (CTR), Emma Stokes WCS; 34-35, Michael Nichols/NGC; 35 (UP CTR), Bruce Dale/NGC; 36, Brent Stirton/GI/NGC; 37, Georgina Gemmell; 38 (LOLE), Lori Epstein/NGC; 38 (LORT), DaddyBit/IS; 38 (UP CTR), Lori Epstein/NGC; 39 (LOLE), Tim Fitzharris; 39 (LORT), Jokia/IS; 40, Lynsey Addario/NGC; 41, naes/IS; 42-43, Deepika Prasad; 43 (LORT), Dr. Amitabh Joshi; 44 (BOTH), Daniel Raven-Ellison; 45 (UPLE), Michael Nichols/NGC; 45 (LORT), Lori Epstein /NGC **CHAPTER 3:** 46-47, Michael Nichols /NGC; 48-49, Michael Nichols /NGC; 50 (LOLE), Michael Nichols/NGC; 50 (LORT), AfriPics.com /Alamy; 50 (UP CTR), Denis-Huot/naturepl.com; 51 (LORT), ivkuzmin/IS; 51 (CTR RT), ElephantVoices; 52 (LO), Terry Biddle; 53, The Elephant Sanctuary in Tennessee; 54-55 (ALL), Michael Nichols/NGC; 56 (UPRT), IFAW, the International Fund for Animal Welfare; 56 (INSET), International Fund for Animal Welfare; 56-57, Patricio Robles Gil/MP/NGC; 58, William Albert Allard/NGC; 59 (CTR LE), Michael Nichols/NGC; 59 (IIPRT), Michael Nichols/NGC; 59 (LORT), Anup Shah/naturepl.com; 59 (LOLE), Ben Osborne/naturepl.com; 60 (LULE), ElephantVoices; 60 (UPRT), Daniel Raven-Ellison; 61, T. N. C. Vidya **CHAPTER 4:** 62-63, Beverly Joubert; 64-65, Michael Nichols/NGC; 66-67, ElephantVoices; 68 (UPRT), Krithi Karanth/CWS; 68 (LOLE), Joel Sartore/NGC; 68 (LORT), Lisa Hoffner/naturepl.com; 69 (LOLE), Jabruson/naturepl.com; 69 (LORT), George F. Mobley/NGC; 70-71, Chris Johns/NGC; 72-73, Beverly Joubert/NGC; 73 (LORT), Beverly Joubert/NGC; 74-75 (ALL), Daniel Raven-Ellison **CHAPTER 5:** 76-77, Tim Fitzharris; 78, Tom Lovell/NGC; 79 (CTR LE), Rutchapong/IS; 79 (UPRT), hnijjar00//IS; 79 (CTR RT), akg-images/Andre Held/Newscom, 79 (LOLE), vasa/Alamy; 80 (UPRT), courtesy Inkamba Nkulu Clement; 80, Michael Nichols/NGC; 81 (UP), Maximilien Bruggmann; 81 (CTR), James P. Blair/NGC; 81 (CTR RT), Victoria Waldock; 82-83, Randy Olson/NGC; 83 (UPRT), Steve Turner/GI; 84 (UPRT), courtesy Inkamba Nkulu Clement; 84-85, Jabruson/naturepl.com; 86-87, Photoshot Holdings Ltd/Alamy; 88, photo courtesy of the Performing Animal Welfare Society—PAWSweb.org; 89, Save Elephant Foundation; 90 (BOTH), Daniel Raven-Ellison; 91, Chris Johns/NGC **CHAPTER 6:** 92-93, Tim Fitzharris; 94-95, Brent Stirton/GI/NGC; 95 (UPLE), Rebecca Hale, NGS; 96 (UPRT), Henry S. Dziekan III/Contributor/GI; 96-97, Tom Stoddart Archive/Contributor/GI; 98 (UPRT), Rebecca Hale, NGS; 98-99, Ariadne Van Zandbergen/Alamy; 99 (LO), HeckerBob/IS; 100, Terry Biddle; 101 (CTR LE), AP Photo/Wally Santana; 101 (UPRT), E Simanor/Alamy; 101 (LORT), Lori Epstein /NGC; 102, IFAW, the International Fund for Animal Welfare; 103, NG PHOTOGRAPHER/NGC; 104 (BOTH), Daniel Raven-Ellison; 105, Michael Nichols/NGC **BACK MATTER:** 106-107, Michael Nichols/NGC; 107 (LORT), David Sheldrick Wildlife Trust; 108 (LORT), Frans Lanting/NGC

>>CREDITS

Thank you to my family—old and new—for your endless love and support.

Special thanks to Kate Olesin, JR Mortimer, and the entire National Geographic Children's Books team, who helped make this book possible.

Daniel Raven-Ellison, Joyce Poole, and all the explorers, researchers, conservationists, and organizations featured in the book—thank you for sharing your stories, photos, and expertise.

Ajay Desai and Bhaskar Krishnamurthy for being my portal into the world of Asian elephants.

And all the passionate people around the world who study elephants and work tirelessly to save them—this book would not have been possible without your efforts. —Ashlee Brown Blewett

For Seb, Menah, Mushroom, and all Earthlings. —Daniel Raven-Ellison

Published by the National Geographic Society

Gary E. Knell, *President and Chief Executive Officer*
John M. Fahey, *Chairman of the Board*
Declan Moore, *Executive Vice President; President, Publishing and Travel*
Melina Gerosa Bellows, *Publisher and Chief Creative Officer, Books, Kids, and Family*

Prepared by the Book Division

Hector Sierra, *Senior Vice President and General Manager*
Nancy Laties Feresten, *Senior Vice President, Kids Publishing and Media*
Jennifer Emmett, *Vice President, Editorial Director, Kids Books*
Eva Absher-Schantz, *Design Director, Kids Publishing and Media*
Jay Sumner, *Director of Photography, Kids Publishing*
R. Gary Colbert, *Production Director*
Jennifer A. Thornton, *Director of Managing Editorial*

Staff for This Book

Kate Olesin, *Editor*
JR Mortimer, *Project Manager*
Julide Dengel, *Art Director*
Graves Fowler Creative, *Designer*
Lori Epstein, *Senior Photo Editor*
Bri Bertoia, *Special Projects Assistant*
Paige Towler, *Editorial Assistant*
Allie Allen, Sanjida Rashid, *Design Production Assistants*
Margaret Leist, *Photo Assistant*
Carl Mehler, *Director of Maps*
Sven M. Dolling, *Map Research and Production*
Grace Hill, *Associate Managing Editor*
Mike O'Connor, *Production Editor*
Lewis R. Bassford, *Production Manager*
Susan Borke, *Legal and Business Affairs*
Scott Elder, *Contributing Writer*

Production Services

Phillip L. Schlosser, *Senior Vice President*
Chris Brown, Vice President, *NG Book Manufacturing*
George Bounelis, *Senior Production Manager*
Nicole Elliott, *Director of Production*
Rachel Faulise, *Manager*
Robert L. Barr, *Manager*

The National Geographic Society is one of the world's largest nonprofit scientific and educational organizations. Founded in 1888 to "increase and diffuse geographic knowledge," the Society's mission is to inspire people to care about the planet. It reaches more than 400 million people worldwide each month through its official journal, *National Geographic*, and other magazines; National Geographic Channel; television documentaries; music; radio; films; books; DVDs; maps; exhibitions; live events; school publishing programs; interactive media; and merchandise. National Geographic has funded more than 10,000 scientific research, conservation, and exploration projects and supports an education program promoting geographic literacy.

For more information, please visit nationalgeographic.com, call 1-800-NGS LINE (647-5463), or write to the following address:
National Geographic Society
1145 17th Street N.W.
Washington, D.C. 20036-4688 U.S.A.

Visit us online at nationalgeographic.com/books

For librarians and teachers: ngchildrensbooks.org

More for kids from National Geographic: kids.nationalgeographic.com

For information about special discounts for bulk purchases, please contact National Geographic Books Special Sales: ngspecsales@ngs.org

For rights or permissions inquiries, please contact National Geographic Books Subsidiary Rights: ngbookrights@ngs.org

Paperback ISBN: 978-1-4263-1729-3
Reinforced library binding ISBN: 978-1-4263-1730-9

Printed in the United States of America

14/WOR/1